BOOK ONE

ART of ATTENTION

BOOK ONE

ART *of* ATTENTION

YOGA WORKBOOK

for teachers and practitioners

ELENA
BROWER

and

ERICA
JAGO

SECOND EDITION

Distributed through Bookmasters.com
Call Toll Free: (877) 312-4094
For International call: (419) 281-5100

To pre-order a copy of the book, visit artofattention.com

Teachings by Elena Brower, transcribed from YogaGlo.com.
Art direction, illustrations and design by Erica Jago.
Photography by: Chapter One and Four // Michael Chichi, Chapter Two // Chloe Crespi,
Chapter Three // Alice Marshall, Chapter Four and Five // Dominic Neitz.
Mandala Artwork by Sofia Escobar.
Portals by Harlan Emil.
Editing and Foreword by Linda Sparrowe.
Printed in Canada by Transcontinental.

Grateful acknowledgement is made to the following
for permission to quote from their works:

From *The Reality of Being*, by Jeanne de Salzmann,
© 2010 by the Heirs of Jeanne de Salzmann.
Reprinted by arrangement with Shambhala Publications Inc., Boston, MA.
www.shambhala.com.

Images of Black Rock City are used at the sole discretion of,
and are the exclusive property of Burning Man.
Reproduction is prohibited. With gratitude for your respect.

ISBN: 978-0-615-66436-1

2012919639

With gratitude to our families, teachers and students.

TABLE OF CONTENTS

Slow everything down in your brain
make space between thoughts and actions

Notice how this increases your sensitivity
keeping you soft

Serving
your family, friends, work

Practice patience in transition
find forgiveness in every context

Emanate consistently
expand consciously

Stay
in the flow

WELCOME

Thank you for holding this in your hands. With this book we hope you take your time, find your own voice in it, ask your questions all over it and make it a home base for your practice and your heart. May these practices remind you that loving yourself is the only prayer, the only practice.

Extend willingness
in all you do

The most spiritual and powerful aspect of human nature is our faculty of attention. **CONSCIOUSNESS.** Attention is what allows us to see ourselves, and see within ourselves, in order to learn how we can elegantly approach anything, everything. Our ability to see ourselves and how we behave is key to harmonizing the dissonance between our inner conversation and our outer conversation, and learning how to love ourselves. May these practices spark that harmony.

To make art of our attention is to be elegant and true to ourselves. So we can be that way for other people. We still don't know how to listen or respond appropriately sometimes. We forget to be grateful. We forget to be soft. This compilation of practices is inspired by several traditions of Hatha yoga, yoga philosophy, Fourth Way teachings and the Handel Method. Each sequence points us toward the inner work of listening, respecting, trusting and healing.

Practice is distilled into three elemental aspects. **SANKALPA** explains the intention for the practice. The **THREE WAVE SEQUENCE** introduces a specific opening into your body through the progression of postures, and the **AWAKENING** pages conclude and close your practice. Pages at the end of each chapter invite your practice notes, intentions and sequences.

Amidst the physical postures and transitions in these practices, we release tension, and find forgiveness. We repattern blame and shame into restful gratitude. We watch our thoughts at a distance, softly separate ourselves from them and consequently see the unity that we are. Rather than blindly hold assumptions, we explore the very highest possibilities in our behavior, our thinking, our commerce. We cultivate an ecology of gratitude in our being, in our home and in our practice. We set an example for everyone around us.

Whether you're a student or a teacher of yoga, you're invited to slow down, reflect and design your experience.

May these practices bring listening, courage and connection.

ELENA AND ERICA

FOREWORD

In ancient times, the physical practice of yoga was a means to control the body and prepare it for the rigors of meditation. Today, asana includes hundreds of postures and represents a body-based meditation designed to help us better understand who we are and how we interact with the world around us. Asana awakens the body, stabilizes and strengthens, softens and opens.

By incorporating the art of attention into our practice, all that bending and stretching, inverting and twisting we call yoga becomes a powerful way to see our minds more clearly and open our hearts more deeply. And that's when magic happens. Bearing witness to our strengths and weaknesses, **WITHOUT JUDGMENT**, allows us to transform our relationship to ourselves into one of loving acceptance and awaken to our innate goodness. These three aspects—physical practice, self-inquiry, and surrender into what yogis call "effortless being"—come together to make yoga first and foremost a spiritual practice.

Together, Elena and Erica weave these concepts into a valuable, artful, and awe-inspiring resource. Through breathtaking photographs, profound insights, and practical step-by-step instruction, they offer students and teachers alike concrete ways to connect with deeper aspects of themselves and emerge more compassionate and more fully engaged in the world. Elena's sequences open and ground the body, placing our attention on what we're most familiar with—the muscles and bones of our being. This disciplined commitment to the physical, known as **TAPAS** in Sanskrit, allows us to access the wisdom of the body; it provides the first step on the path toward trusting, respecting, and ultimately healing ourselves. In concert with Erica's masterful design, Elena's instructions and inquiries invite us to take action, on our mats and in our lives. Together they give us the blueprint we need to initiate that healing.

As we become more aware of our physical form, we're asked to identify and reflect on our actions. This concept of **SVADHYAYA** — self-awareness — helps us notice patterns and habits that have kept us stuck in discomfort. It allows us to approach them from a place of acceptance instead of judgment. The sequences and meditation techniques help us let go of blame and other self-destructive thoughts and emotions that no longer serve us. By forgiving ourselves and others, we can then dissolve any sense of separateness we experience.

When we let go of our fears and insecurities and embrace our true nature, we learn what it means to be fully alive. In this act of surrender, **ISHVARA PRANIDHANA**, we cultivate a mind that allows us to see the divine essence in all beings, including ourselves. Through the clarity of the practices shared, we are implored to live our yoga in everything we do, give up our attachment to a future outcome and reside with gratitude in the present moment.

I encourage you to sit with this book and experience its gifts. The imagery and design will inspire you to dance your yoga, luxuriating in the transition from one pose to the next. You'll find Erica's sequence drawings and Elena's succinct reminders throughout the book to be invaluable teaching tools. And when you finish the last chapter, you'll thank these remarkable women for the spirit of their collaboration, evidenced in these pages, which captures the true meaning of yoga in such an exquisite, heart-opening way.

LINDA SPARROWE
EDITOR IN CHIEF, YOGA INTERNATIONAL

MC YOGI

FORGIVENESS DOESN'T ALWAYS HAPPEN RIGHT AWAY, BUT THE PROCESS CAN BEGIN IMMEDIATELY. Actively engaging in the forgiveness process begins our journey toward deeper understanding, and the remembrance that everything happens for a reason. When we're able to extract wisdom from our past dramas and traumas, we're able to gain direct knowledge. Looking back, we can become grateful for the things that happened to us in the past, for helping us to grow and become more aware.

The art of attention and the cultivation of compassion can often take a great deal of work, but it's important to remember that this work is extremely rewarding. When we forgive, we feel ten times lighter. We're able to think and see more clearly, and we can gain greater access to the storehouse of energy that's inside us (and all around us). Energy that was once being consumed by the past can now become an open resource (re-Source) for living more fully in the present.

When we forgive ourselves and others, the entire orchestrated universe conspires to help support our healing process.

The forgiveness process can also be very humbling; we know that there's most likely someone out there who needs to forgive us as well.

When we start to gather wisdom from our experiences, the yogis suggest that this process is similar to a bee that gathers pollen to make nectar. The bee is said to take a little poison along with the pollen, and when it's brought to the hive, it's carefully transformed into nectar. Learning to turn a negative situation into pure wisdom is an indication that we are progressing in our yoga and meditation practices. As we become more skillful agents of love and compassion, the heavy load that we've lugged around in the back of our mind begins to soften, and gradually dissolves. When we're able to reach the place of gratitude in our forgiveness process, we'll know we've made it through to the other side.

Forgiveness is the attribute of the strong.

MAHATMA GANDHI

YOU ARE INVITED TO TRANSFORM TENSION INTO FORGIVENESS.

CHAPTER ONE

REDUCE TENSION & FIND FORGIVENESS

photography by MICHAEL CHICHI

Fast-paced flow sequence; focus on increasing speed and stability while decreasing tension in your body. Applicable to your poses, interactions and relationships, this sequence will make you feel more porous, lighter, stronger, softer and more forgiving of yourself and others.

I forgive, heal and release everything that consciously or unconsciously could delay or block the complete evolution of my being.

– MARIO LIANI –

SANKALPA

WELCOME, TAKE A NICE SEAT.

Close your eyes, rest your hands on your thighs and bring your chin to your chest. This is a sequence of flowing, delicious, increasing speed. We are practicing how to increase speed while decreasing tension in the body.

Once there was a man who described painting houses during his teens with his father, who was an expert house painter. His father was in his 60s, more than three times his son's age, yet was able to work twice as fast. The son asked his father how he was able to work so quickly and efficiently; his father replied that he had learned to increase his speed while decreasing tension in his body.

There are definitive turning points in our days, in our poses, in our thoughts, when we can choose to turn the tension level down, even amidst an increase in velocity.

Practice this; feel sharp, more awake, more porous, more lit up, be spacious enough to stay forgiving, no matter the context.

Fold your hands in front of your heart.
Call to your heart, connect to your heart and slow it down.

If at anytime you feel disconnected,
that is your sign that you are longing for more connection.

Inhale deeply.

OM NAMAH SHIVAYA

I bow to my deepest heart

Bring your chin to your chest. Stay close to yourself throughout
the practice, no matter how quickly you move. The closer you stay
to yourself, the less contraction you'll experience, and the more
connected and forgiving you'll feel.

REDUCE TENSION AND FIND FORGIVENESS

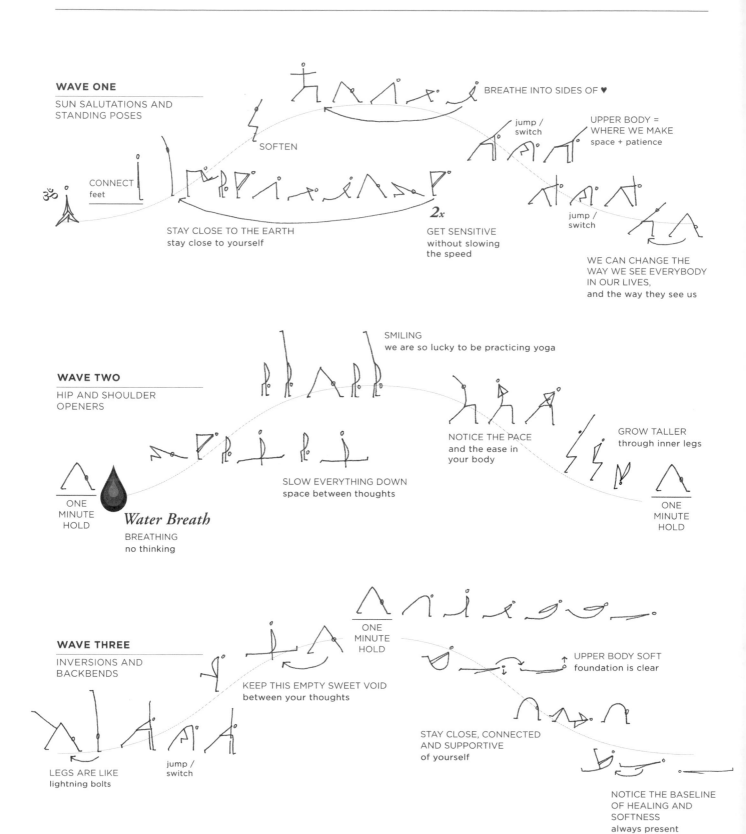

WAVE ONE

SUN SALUTATIONS AND
STANDING POSES

BREATHE INTO SIDES OF ♥

jump /
switch

UPPER BODY =
WHERE WE MAKE
space + patience

SOFTEN

CONNECT
feet

STAY CLOSE TO THE EARTH
stay close to yourself

2x

GET SENSITIVE
without slowing
the speed

jump /
switch

WE CAN CHANGE THE
WAY WE SEE EVERYBODY
IN OUR LIVES,
and the way they see us

WAVE TWO

HIP AND SHOULDER
OPENERS

SMILING
we are so lucky to be practicing yoga

NOTICE THE PACE
and the ease in
your body

GROW TALLER
through inner legs

ONE
MINUTE
HOLD

Water Breath

BREATHING
no thinking

SLOW EVERYTHING DOWN
space between thoughts

ONE
MINUTE
HOLD

WAVE THREE

INVERSIONS AND
BACKBENDS

ONE
MINUTE
HOLD

KEEP THIS EMPTY SWEET VOID
between your thoughts

UPPER BODY SOFT
foundation is clear

STAY CLOSE, CONNECTED
AND SUPPORTIVE
of yourself

LEGS ARE LIKE
lightning bolts

jump /
switch

NOTICE THE BASELINE
OF HEALING AND
SOFTNESS
always present

*Begin at the top
of your mat*

palms facing forward

TADASANA | MOUNTAIN POSE

Close your eyes and feel where there is tension in your body.
Soften your toes; breathe into the back of your belly.

2x

SURYA NAMASKARA A | SUN SALUTATION

Reduce the tension

without slowing
the speed

Become more sensitive to your own breathing. Send your breath to
the spaces in your body that need your attention the most; this will
have the effect of slowing down time. Our aim is to slow ourselves
down enough to truly listen to what is going on - to the people
around us, and to ourselves at the deepest level.

Be sensitive

without slowing
the speed

SOFTEN

UTKATASANA | CHAIR

Soften your eyeballs, the sockets of your eyes and the spaces behind your eyes. Soften your thighbones down into your groins, soften the back of your belly and lift it gently up towards your lungs. Spread your collarbones wide to the sides.

Stay

close to the earth

Stay

close to yourself

VIRABHADRASANA II | WARRIOR II

Practice reverence here. Even as you expand through every limb in every direction, close your eyes, soften your skin and let there be reverence. Reverence is a form of respectful listening, a sensitivity to all that is. Your listening is what stops contractions of any kind in your body, in any way – cellularly, muscularly, in your nervous system – allowing you to stay in the flow of the present moment.

Listening stops contractions

in the cells, in the muscles, in the nervous system

Reverence

is a form of listening

Your legs are, at all times, sturdy, steady, concentrated and earthy. The rest of your body is open, sweet, soft, listening and reverent.

Bend your front knee more deeply by bringing the middle of your front seat all the way beneath you. On your front leg, lift the inner thigh up and around to your outer thigh. Bend your front knee a little more deeply. Feel for any place in your body where there is tension. Soften; keep your legs strong.

jump switch

UTTHITA PARSVAKONASANA | SIDE ANGLE

Place your fingertips on the little toe side of your front foot. Press your front knee into your upper arm; this stabilizing point of contact helps you wrap your front seat underneath you more deeply. Nikki Costello, my Iyengar teacher, offers this subtle yet structurally empowering distinction: *keep the outer pad of your back foot rooted down into the floor, and feel the inner edge of the outer pad of your foot.* To connect to your foundation in this way grants access to the back of your body, opening your heart. It makes us softer, more sensitive without losing groundedness or strength. Bend your front knee more deeply, breathe into the back of your belly, and curl into a slight backbend as you lengthen your tailbone down and beneath you. Expand energy from your hips outward. Soften your eyes.

When you're ready, jump to switch your feet.

Cultivate pure strength and stability in the lower half of your body. Practice complete listening, space and patience in the upper half.

Upper body = where we make
space + patience

Grant access
3 to the back of your body

Upper arm + outer knee
1 points of contact

Press-down
2 the inner edge of the outer pad of foot

jump switch

UTTHITA TRIKONASANA | TRIANGLE

Hug your feet in energetically toward one another. As though drawing a line upward, lift up from your inner heels to your inner groins, and move your inner, uppermost groins back and wide. Lengthen your tailbone down. Curl your upper body softly and respectfully back. Lift your lower belly away from the floor and receive your breathing for a few breaths. Then bend your front knee deeply and jump to switch the feet.

See the beauty in this transition as you jump to switch your feet.

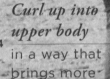

Curl up into upper body
4 in a way that brings more softness

Upper, inner groins back
2 and wide

Lengthen
3 tailbone down

Draw a line
1 up inner heel to inner groin

When we pay attention, we more readily feel the ground beneath us. Begin to hear everyone, anyone, without imposing assumptions or opinions, from a stable, receptive place.

ASHVA SANCHALANASANA | GALLOPING HORSE

Long trajectory forward, stay strong through your legs and get softer in your upper body.

We can change the way we see
everybody in our lives,
and the way they see us

ONE
MINUTE
HOLD

ADHO MUKHA SHVANASANA | DOWNWARD FACING DOG

Strong legs; send your upper inner and outer thighs back.

Notice how this increases your sensitivity keeping you soft

Your mouth is slightly open, just barely parting your lips.

WATER BREATH
by
SALLY KEMPTON

UTTANASANA | STANDING FORWARD FOLD
HANUMANASANA | SPLITS

From Uttanasana, step your left foot all the way to the back of your mat; and shimmy your front foot all the way to the front of your mat. Pause. Almost in Hanumanasana, splits pose, hug your feet energetically toward one another, creating strength and clarity. Then fold your upper body forward onto your front leg and expand softly outward through both legs.

Hold for five to ten breaths, then switch sides.

THE DISTINCTION: Soften your face and your neck. Dare to do this in your conversations; hold your ground but be very receptive. Listen. You will have the same reaction over and over unless you know where your ground is. **PRACTICE TRUSTING:** Soften your upper body to receive this understanding. Every single one of us has the capacity to "see" beyond what our senses perceive; with this practice we get quiet enough to do so.

Your legs have never been stronger

and your upper body has never been softer

Smiling
we are so lucky to be
able to practice yoga

URDHVA PRASARITA EKA PADASANA | STANDING SPLITS
ADHO MUKHA SHVANASANA | DOWNWARD FACING DOG

Step one foot forward, lift your other leg high, and flex your top foot.
Press the ball of your top foot up. Hold the back of your standing heel
with your hand. Lengthen the top leg upward from your inner thigh to
the inner heel, and draw the top of your head in towards your standing
shin. Soften the features of your face and receive your breathing
throughout your upper body.

Breathe several breaths, and then switch sides.

PARIVRITTA ANJANEYASANA WITH ANJALI MUDRA |
HIGH LUNGE TWIST WITH HANDS TO HEART

From Downward Facing Dog, step one foot forward and come
up to High Lunge. Inhale arms up, exhale hands to prayer. Take
a deep breath to make space inside and twist to your front leg
side, opposite elbow outside your front knee. Hug your back foot
and front foot together, lift your back leg inner thigh. Get softer
in your upper body so you can receive another full breath in your
top lung, then twist from your bottom lung as you expand from
your hips out through your feet, decreasing tension. Notice the
pace and the ease in your body for two more breaths.

*Release hands to floor, Downward Facing Dog, and
do your second side.*

UTKATASANA | CHAIR TO UTTANASANA |
STANDING FORWARD FOLD WITH HANDS INTERLACED

Interlace your hands behind you to open up your shoulders.
Bring your hands closer to one another. Breathe space between
your integrated shoulderblades, behind your heart. Breathe three
to five breaths; become more integrated and softer. Exhale to
fold down; bring your arms up and over your head. Straighten
your legs, relax your toes. Lift from your inner heels to your inner
knees up to your inner groins; grow taller through your inner
legs. Lengthen the space between your inner knees and your
inner thighs, to stabilize your sacrum and receive more breath
and space in your lower spine.

Taller

through inner legs

*Breathe deeply five to ten breaths, then release your
hands down to the ground.*

ADHO MUKHA SHVANASANA | DOWNWARD FACING DOG

ONE MINUTE HOLD

Your hands are part of your foundation; keep your hands and arms strong, your internal organs soft and spacious. Inspired by dear friend and colleague Christina Sell, enjoy a one-minute down dog, As you breathe there, ask - can I get softer in my brain, my eyes, my heart?

VRKSASANA | HANDSTAND

Go to the wall, or work in the middle of the room. Keep your arms strong, your legs strong and your foundation clear. Soften your organs, your belly, your face. Keep your legs and arms strong so the rest of your body can receive your breathing.

Legs are like

lightning bolts

jump switch

Breathing

thinking spaciously

PARIVRITTA ANJANEYASANA | HIGH LUNGE TWIST

From Downward Facing Dog, step your right foot outside your right hand and raise your right arm high to the sky. Keeping your legs strong, fill both lungs, stay soft interiorly. Lift your top lung to twist your bottom lung forward and up for 5 breaths, expanding from your hips out through your feet, no tension in your body.

Return to Downward Facing Dog, switch to step your left foot forward, left arm high.

BAKASANA | CROW

Keep your lungs open and receptive in Downward Facing Dog. Walk your feet forward to place your knees onto your upper arms, then walk your feet together behind you on the floor until your big toes touch. Breathe into the backs of your lungs, squeeze your knees into your upper arms; exhale your heart and gaze forward. Inhale again, hug your knees in, lift your feet as you round your back slightly. Exhale to lift your feet and seat higher, send your gaze and heart forward, take two more spacious breaths.

Keep this empty sweet void
between your thoughts

keep your organs and your upper body open and listening

Return to Downward Facing Dog.

SECOND TIME

HANUMANASANA | SPLITS

From Downward Facing Dog, place one foot between your hands. Notice the anticipation, the speed in your mind. Slow everything down in your brain; put a space between this thought and the next. As you hug your feet towards each other, do so patiently; contract and release - feet in, feet out to lengthen your legs - but notice the patience possible in that process. Widen your back seat out, wrap your front seat beneath you - lift that side from lower belly to lung - and exhale from your hips to lengthen your legs longer. Feel patience in your entire body.

Return to Downward Facing Dog, switch sides.

Slow everything down in your brain
make space between thoughts and actions

Invite more patience into your upper body as you make the effort to strengthen and expand. Amidst moments of effort and velocity, interior patience yields, for ourselves and others, potent forgiveness.

We are reducing tension within our architectural form. We are cultivating space in which to find forgiveness.

Return to Downward Facing Dog.

ONE
MINUTE
HOLD

ADHO MUKHA SHVANASANA | DOWNWARD FACING DOG

Strong foundation, strong limbs, super soft heart, belly, kidneys. Make your inner body more porous, more expansive. Notice the quality of attention, of acceptance, of forgiveness that wells up in your heart and send that light down your arms out to your hands, and to your hips, down your legs, to your feet.

*Practice
patience
in transition*

find forgiveness
in every context

DOWNWARD FACING DOG > PLANK POSE >
UPWARD FACING DOG > COBRA > LOCUST

From Downward Facing Dog, keep your arms straight,
curl forward into Upward Facing Dog.

Bend your elbows to lower your ribs down into Cobra,
and then lower your chest onto the floor;
Lift your upper arms into small Cobra,
expand your chest out to the sides.

Keep your upper body exactly as it is, slightly lifted.
Interlace your hands behind you for Locust.

Now from the very top of your thighs,
right where your thighs meet your hips,
lift your legs up off the floor.
Lift from your thighs, then
lift your feet.

Feel the effort, the speed;
decrease any remaining interior tension with your breathing.

Hug your knees toward one another and bring your feet closer.
Keeping your neck long and your eyes soft,
Lift your upper arm bones and head high, away from the floor.

Lengthen your tailbone long toward your heels; soften your kidneys and
adrenals to open your entire upper body even as you lift strongly.

Keep your tailbone long and invite your breathing into your lower back,
connect to yourself with full acceptance.

Take five breaths
with soft eyes.

Gently release down
and rest, with your head to one side.

DHANURASANA | UPWARD BOW

Bend your knees; reach back to hold your feet. Bring your knees closer together. Forehead on or near the floor. Breathe into your heart circumferentially, all the way up underneath your collarbones, down into your lower belly. Lift the tops of your thighs. At the same time and with the same velocity, lengthen your tailbone towards the back of your mat, knees stay parallel, so that your legs are clearly strong but lengthening as well.

Lift up and back through your thighs, your knees, your feet. Receive your own breathing for 5 breaths, then gently release down. Turn your gaze to one side, palms facing up next to your hips.

Feel the quality of patient forgiveness coursing through your body as you rest.

THE DISTINCTION: See in your physical body the presence of both groundedness (the drawing in) and complete acceptance (the opening/lengthening). In our interactions, our relationships, our ways of communicating with the people near us, we can apply both qualities. There are some people with whom we should be more grounded, more stable. There are others in our lives with whom we are perhaps unable to listen, everything inside contracts and speeds up when we're in their presence - with them we can be more receptive, and cultivate a quality of opening, of allowance, of acceptance. In both cases, even as things get amplified or hastened, we can reduce the tension in our bodies and generate profound healings.

Where you feel the most resistance is where you can place your attention. Listen for those little resistances, they are your map, telling you where you can put more of your steadiness or more of your listening.

Take five breaths here

lower down to rest

SUPTA TADASANA | RECLINED MOUNTAIN

Roll over onto your back. With your legs long and straight, flex your feet, root your thighbones down, feel the earth beneath you. Draw energy up - ground to inner heels, up into inner knees, up to inner thighs. Then root your inner thighs down, inner knees down, inner heels down. Simultaneously root your outer hips, your outer knees, your outer heels. Maintain your strong, deliberately grounded legs, toes pointing skyward, and notice how the rest of your body opens. **SPACIOUS. RECEIVING.**

Keep that awareness and bend your knees to place your feet on the ground to prepare for Urdhva Dhanurasana.

URDHVA DHANURASANA | FULL WHEEL

Place your hands by your ears, and bend your knees to place your feet on the floor. Draw energy up from your inner heels, to your inner knees, to your inner thighs, and then root back down into the floor. With strong legs, lift up into full wheel, and gently send your heart over your wrists. Lengthen your legs, press your feet down and soften your whole upper body to receive your breathing. Take three steady, open breaths, slow down especially when it feels rushed in your body - as though things are moving too quickly on the deepest levels.

Gently lower down. Rest with your knees together, feet apart.

Every time we do the poses themselves with intention, we heal generations of haste, fear, tension and disconnection. This healing is true, it's happening right now, in our bodies as we read and practice, in our minds as we consider the possibilities. In honour of all the people who've preceded you, make space for patience, for release, for the most profoundly healing acceptance.

SECOND TIME: Place your hands to come up. Reiterate the strength in your legs and arms as well as the sweetness and open receptivity in your listening heart.

Stay close, connected and supportive of yourself

SUPTA PADANGUSTHASANA |
RECLINED LEG STRETCH

Lengthen your legs long on the floor, flex your feet. Root one thigh down into the floor strongly and bend your other knee into your chest. Interlace your hands behind the hamstrings of your top leg, close to your groin. Lengthen that leg high and long to the sky. Bend your elbows to peel your back off the floor, and lift your nose all the way up to your lifted shin. Stay strong in both legs and soften your face, your neck and your shoulders. Extend from your pelvis out through both feet for a few more breaths, then release down slowly.

Rest for two to three breaths. When you feel ready, switch sides.

We are cultivating a certain consistency, so no matter what the circumstance, your upper body is soft, and your foundation is clear, holding stillness. Reduce tension and move towards forgiveness, no matter the context.

Upper body soft
foundation is clear

SHAVASANA | CORPSE

Lie flat. Place your hands on your body as you wish; we love left hand to heart, right hand to belly. If your mind is still rushing, keep your left hand on your heart and place your right hand on the top of your head, with your elbow resting on the floor – to breathe space between your thoughts.

Rest.

Notice the baseline of healing and softness always present

AWAKENING

Very gently begin to deepen your breathing.

Slowly draw your knees into your chest.

Come up to sitting through your right side.

Fold your hands in front of your heart in prayer.

Our ability to increase speed while decreasing tension is an art. This practice helps us create the spaciousness we need within ourselves to find the art, in both the speed *and* the calm, throughout our lives.

Practice it on yourself
silently in your own heart
say at least twice

"I forgive, heal and release everything that consciously or unconsciously could delay or block the complete evolution of my being."

– MARIO LIANI

To all of our teachers, to our family and to the ways in which we can bring patience and forgiveness to every realm, every moment of our lives.

NAMASTE.

SANKALPA

I FEEL
STRONGLY THAT
ALL THOSE WHO
ARE THINKING IN
TERMS OF THE
NEW HARMONY
SHOULD KNOW
AND RECOGNIZE
EACH OTHER,
AT LEAST BY
NAME AND
PERSONALLY
IF POSSIBLE.
THEIR COMMON
RECOGNITION
OF EACH
OTHER AND
OF A GREAT
PLAN FAR
ABOVE THEM
ALL MAKES A
POSITIVE FIELD
OF FORCE IN
WHICH MANY
THINGS ARE
POSSIBLE.

- RODNEY COLLIN

FROM DEFENSES TO SOFTNESS

TALKING POINTS

STAY CLOSE TO YOURSELF.

REVERENCE IS A FORM OF LISTENING.

TALKING POINTS

USE YOUR BEAUTY TO SERVE OTHERS IN FINDING THEIR OWN BEAUTY.

AIM:

WAVE ONE

WAVE TWO

WAVE THREE

AWAKENING

THE LAW OF MAINTENANCE:
**WHAT GOES UNFED WEAKENS,
WHAT YOU FEED GROWS STRONGER.**

- RED HAWK

GABRIELLE BERNSTEIN

AS A SPIRITUAL STUDENT AND TEACHER, I'VE COME TO ACCEPT THAT SELF-COMPASSION AND FORGIVENESS ARE MY GREATEST VIRTUES. If we want to grow spiritually we must live from a place of non-judgment and release blame toward others and ourselves.

The practice begins with ourselves. Blame and judgment are the ego's tricks for keeping us stuck in the illusory world of fear. It's easy to stay stuck in the past, wishing we could have done things differently, wishing we could be different. But we must accept that the past no longer exists and that the present is an opportunity for spiritual growth and healing. Releasing self-blame is a fierce commitment to self-love. It immediately unleashes us from our past and centers us into the present.

The practice
begins with ourselves

As spiritual students, we must stretch beyond our limiting beliefs and heighten our awareness of the love that dwells in our most silent moments. We must center into our innocence to move beyond blame.

As we look at our fear through loving lenses, we must be a non-judgmental witness of our ego's tricks. Simple awareness is all we need to look and let go. As teachers, we use our fear as a learning device for self-love, awareness and great new lessons to share with our students.

*Art of Attention ignites
the presence of peace, stillness
and full self-acceptance.*

This is what this book
is teaching us

Let the coming practice help
you flow through any lingering
self-blame. Center into your
innocence, forgive yourself
and awaken your loving truth.
To teach love you must dwell
in a space of love.

YOU ARE INVITED TO RELEASE AND
MOVE BEYOND BLAME.

CHAPTER TWO

LET GO OF BLAME

photography by CHLOE CRESPI

This restorative sequence is about releasing blame from your body and life, restoring your innate power to see yourself, and creating a more cohesive unity in your being. Beginning with four standing poses, you'll move through a round of very restful postures to bring you home to your heart.

The sense of my life today is to be entirely available to the immaterial Presence in me through a state in which I will be completely passive and yet very awake. This requires a balance between the intensity of presence and a greater and greater relaxation.

– THE REALITY OF BEING: THE FOURTH WAY OF GURDJIEFF
   BY MADAME JEANNE DE SALZMANN

Get creative in how you support yourself

Select a couple of pillows, towels, blankets and bolsters

SANKALPA

WELCOME. TAKE A COMFORTABLE SEAT.

Rest your hands on your thighs and close your eyes. Invite your intention to release all blame. Settle into your seat, lean back into your sitting bones and from the stability of your seat, rise up.

Begin to deepen your breathing. Take a complete look, get a full impression of everything about yourself and your context right now.

One of my most treasured books is The Reality of Being: The Fourth Way of Gurdjieff by Jeanne de Salzmann. Madame de Salzmann was a direct student of Gurdjieff. In her own work, she constantly asked herself if she could be more present, more active (and not continually occupied with her memory) in order to respond to anything that happens. Her consistent question to herself: Can I be more active, more present, more attentive to what is really happening, rather than to my memories or projections?

Such thinking would hold itself in front of a fact, sensitive and receptive, without making any judgment or suggestion, without any thoughts. It would hold itself simply by an urgency to know the truth. This thinking would be like a light. It would be able to see.

THE REALITY of BEING
The Fourth Way of Gurdjieff

So as you sit, can you gain an "impression," a mental picture, of where you are right now in this moment? Can you hold yourself, and place your attention, "in front of" what is currently happening instead of what has already happened?

Fold your hands in front of your heart in prayer, and come to a moment of presence with yourself that is attentive, aware and complete.

Exhale. The impression to take of your state during this class, or in any moment, is not as fixed as a photograph. But each time you watch yourself and you learn what is animating you and acting on you, you gain magnetism, power, strength, mastery. *It has nothing to do with power **over** other people. It has everything to do with being extremely aware of yourself, of who and how you are.* Again, ask what acts on you, what animates you? Throughout the class, take those **SNAPSHOTS** of who - and how - you are. Stand in front of your memories - don't let them steer you. You create an entirely new picture, every moment. This is the magic of being human.

Inhale deeply.

ॐ

Let that sound
resonate in your heart

LET GO OF BLAME

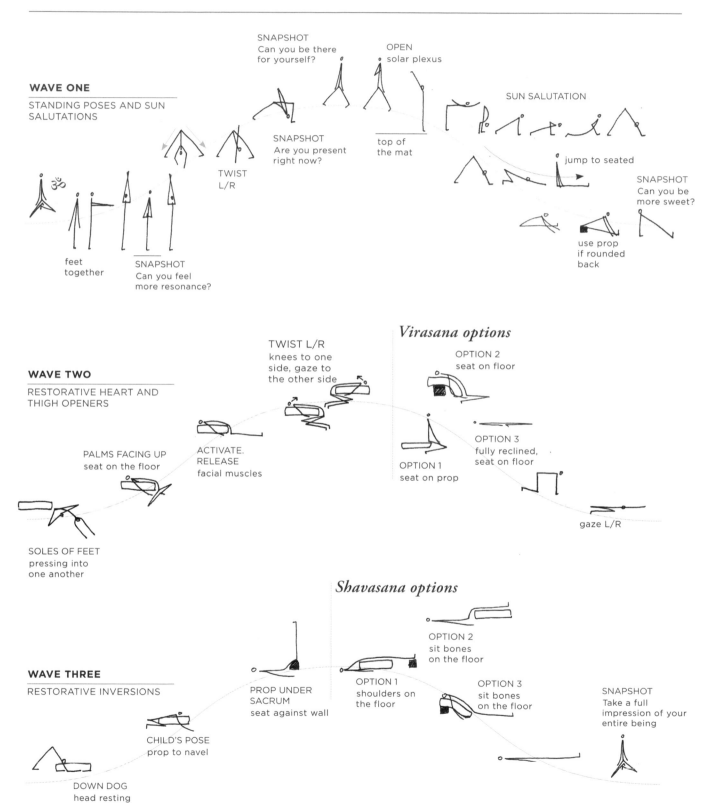

WAVE ONE

STANDING POSES AND SUN SALUTATIONS

SNAPSHOT
Can you be there for yourself?

SNAPSHOT
Are you present right now?

OPEN
solar plexus

SUN SALUTATION

top of the mat

jump to seated

SNAPSHOT
Can you be more sweet?

TWIST L/R

use prop if rounded back

feet together

SNAPSHOT
Can you feel more resonance?

WAVE TWO

RESTORATIVE HEART AND THIGH OPENERS

TWIST L/R
knees to one side, gaze to the other side

Virasana options

OPTION 2
seat on floor

OPTION 3
fully reclined, seat on floor

OPTION 1
seat on prop

PALMS FACING UP
seat on the floor

ACTIVATE.
RELEASE
facial muscles

gaze L/R

SOLES OF FEET
pressing into one another

Shavasana options

OPTION 2
sit bones on the floor

WAVE THREE

RESTORATIVE INVERSIONS

PROP UNDER SACRUM
seat against wall

OPTION 1
shoulders on the floor

OPTION 3
sit bones on the floor

SNAPSHOT
Take a full impression of your entire being

CHILD'S POSE
prop to navel

DOWN DOG
head resting on prop

URDHVA BADDHA HASTASANA |
UPWARD BOUND HAND POSE

Stand at the front of your mat; palms facing forward, feet touching. Lift the sides of your waist and the back of your heart away from the floor as you inhale; reach your arms up to the sky. Breathe there, interlace your hands above your head; stretch long and tall, exhale. Feel into your body as you take this momentary **SNAPSHOT** of where you are. Notice any spaces in your body that feel closed, and send your breathing - the light of your attention - there.

Release your hands into prayer and close your eyes for a moment. Feel the resonance of that stretch in your shoulders and upper arms and heart.

SNAPSHOT

Can you feel more resonance?

After a couple of breaths, switch the cross of your hands to the non-habitual interlacing, bring your hands up overhead and turn them inside out, palms facing the ceiling.

Root your feet down into the floor. Feel the connection of your two sides. This should feel very stabilizing.

Lower your arms, fold your hands back into prayer in front of your heart, and close your eyes. It takes only seconds to bring us into our hearts, to feel more resonance and connection to ourselves. Once again, take a **SNAPSHOT** of your interior space; how you feel inside.

Gently release your hands.

TWIST
L/R

PRASARITA PADOTTANASANA |
WIDE-LEGGED FORWARD BEND

Step your feet wide on your mat, parallel your
feet and face one side of your mat. Hug your
feet in towards one another until you feel
your inner thigh muscles hugging onto your
thighbones, then fold down deeply. Bring your
chin to chest and the top of your head towards
the floor. If your head touches the floor, bring
your feet a little closer together so that you
have to reach for that connection.

Line up your hands so that your fingertips
and your toe tips are in line, bend your elbows
and draw the top of your head down toward
the floor. From your pelvis, expand down,
grounding into your feet. Open up your organs
to clear internally for a few breaths. Come up
to your fingertips, walk your hands out in front
of you, come up onto the fingertips of your left
hand and bring your right arm high to the sky
for the twist.

SNAPSHOT

Breathe and lengthen your tailbone long, take a little **SNAPSHOT** here: Are you *with* your breathing? Are you present; are you here?

Lower your right hand to the floor.

Are you present, truly here? Come up onto your right hand fingertips; inhale your left arm high to the sky. Land yourself in your feet, take a nice full breath and be there for yourself the same way that you would want your best friend to be there for you.

You are home.

Gently release your left hand to the floor and interlace both hands behind your back; reach your interlaced hands up to draw yourself up to stand. Keep your legs strong and feet clear.

Feel your heart.

HUMBLE
WARRIOR
L/R

BADDHA VIRABHADRASANA |
HUMBLE WARRIOR

Turn towards your left foot. Turn that foot to
face forward, and reach your right heel back
behind you, bend your front knee deeply.
Warrior I, hands still interlaced behind you.

To open your hips, bring your left shoulder to
the inside of your left knee and fold; bring your
arms up over your head. Keep your back foot
strong on the floor, back leg straight. Bend
your front knee deeply down. Lift up from your
inner knees to your inner groins. Lengthen
your tailbone long towards the floor and root
down from your inner knees to your inner heels.
Inhale come all the way up to stand, straighten
your front leg.

Switch to face your right leg.

This is the strongest pose of this practice. Bend your right knee deeply. Bring your right shoulder to the inside of your right knee; bring the top of your head down towards the floor, inside your right foot. Bend your front knee deeply. Inhale lift up from your inner knees to your inner groins; root down from your inner knees down to your inner heels. Lengthen your tailbone long to the floor. Hands above your head, breathing deeply. Take a **SNAPSHOT**: How are you with yourself here? Are you here for yourself; or can you be here more fully? Bend your front knee even more deeply, breathing.

Strong legs, strong feet, inhale come up to standing.

SNAPSHOT

Are you present for yourself, here?

SOLAR PLEXUS

Turn your feet parallel. Release your hands and let your arms dangle down at your sides for a moment. Close your eyes and breathe. Feel the space you've created in your shoulders, and the back of your neck.

Press your index fingers into your solar plexus and open there. Especially if you spend any time being angry with yourself. It's healing to breathe open that space where your bottom ribs meet. Hold your attention in that space, release your hands down and breathe there for a few moments.

If it feels elusive to you to open and breathe into your solar plexus, lean back into your heels, and arch back into a gentle backbend. Lift your middle and upper spine, and stay tall as you lean through the sides of your neck. Keep your thighbones back, lean into your back body, and soften your face. Breathe a few breaths here, then gently lift your back ribs to come back to standing. Pause to feel the interior release and opening in your upper body.

Jump your feet together and come to stand at the front of your mat.

top of
the mat

jump through to
seated

SURYA NAMASKARA A | SUN SALUTATION

Inhale reach up, exhale fold down. Inhale your heart forward, exhale smoothly back to Chaturanga Dandasana. Inhale to Upward Facing Dog, exhale to Downward Facing Dog.

Take a little hold in Downward Facing Dog for just a few moments. From your hands and your feet draw energy up from the earth into your heart. Fill your heart with your breathing. With strong arms extend from your heart back down through your hands; down through your feet.

Slowly bend your knees, look between your hands and jump all the way through to sitting.

Extend your legs out.

SNAPSHOT

Can you be there for yourself?

use prop if
rounded back

PASCHIMOTTANASANA |
SEATED FORWARD BEND

From Dandasana, sitting tall, use your hands to root your inner legs down, seat out and wide. Then root your outer legs down. Keep props close if you have them, and bring your hands to either side of your shins. Reach your sitting bones back and wide as much as you can, and sit up as tall as possible.

If your lower back cannot lengthen upright here, place a blanket, folded towel or pillow beneath your seat to lift your hips. More circulation in your lower back nourishes your adrenals and kidneys in the pose.

Gently fold your upper body over your legs, keeping your legs grounded, feet flexed.

The point of a restorative practice is to literally feed our organs with the kind of patience and restfulness that we do not normally afford our bodies. Keep your hands on the floor regardless of your flexibility. Our aim is to be more grounded through our legs, so we can be fully present, before reaching forward.

Madame de Salzmann compares the impressions we take in every moment with the food that we eat. Each impression, whether we are taking a **SNAPSHOT** of ourselves or observing any experience, brings an energy to us that must be received.

Spend a few breaths or several minutes here, then slowly come up.

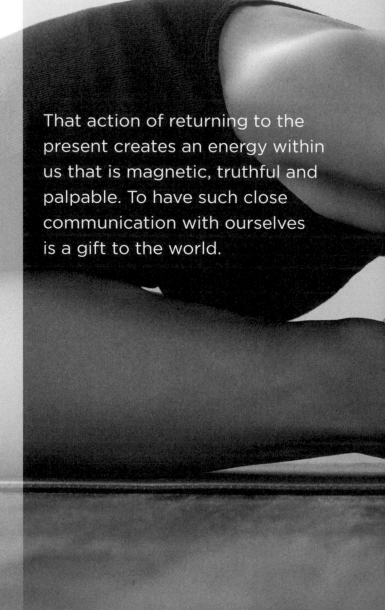

That action of returning to the present creates an energy within us that is magnetic, truthful and palpable. To have such close communication with ourselves is a gift to the world.

SNAPSHOT

How are you with *yourself* here?
May you be patient, loving,
attentive, accepting.

PURVOTTANASANA | UPWARD PLANK POSE

Circle your arms up and back behind you, place
your hands down and turn your fingers to face
forward and slightly out to the side. Point your
toes, lift your pelvis, lengthen up into your
shoulders and breathe deeply as you point your
toes down to the floor.

*Breathe for three to five breaths and observe
the interior opening. Gently release.*

SOLES OF FEET
pressing into
one another

BADDHA KONASANA | BOUND ANGLE

Bring the soles of your feet to touch in Baddha Konasana. Place your bolster, folded blankets, couch cushion or two firm pillows directly behind your seat, lengthwise. Slowly fold yourself forward into Baddha Konasana. Press your feet into one another, widen your seat back behind you, and slowly fold down. Be clear with yourself and breathe directly into your boundary here, without trying to change anything.

When we start to try and fix things - a very human and habitual choice - we lose contact with reality. Whatever it is that you are managing today, see it, observe it; all of its facets, aspects, weirdness and wonderfulness.

The moment you see it without trying to fix it, THAT is consciousness. And in that moment, there is a solution lingering in your observation.

Slowly inhale up.

PALMS FACING UP
seat on the floor

SUPTA BADDHA KONASANA |
RECLINED BOUND ANGLE

Keeping your feet in Baddha Konasana, come to lie back on your bolster. Your seat is on the floor, your back is lying on the bolster. You are well supported here; this should feel as though you are reclining, very restfully.

Welcome yourself here.

Anytime you feel like you are separate, not a unity, as though you can't be conscious because there is a distraction, remember the power and magic of being human: in any moment, you can choose to be fully conscious of exactly where you stand, exactly how things are, and exactly what you can do to make space within yourself in order to manage the current reality.

In that space is every solution.

This is more about observing
and less about fixing

Take at least two minutes
to rest here.

ACTIVATE.
RELEASE
facial muscles

Stay on your bolster and lengthen your legs out in front of you. With eyes closed, open the muscles of your face. Keeping your eyes closed, open and close your mouth. Open and stretch your face and jaw as much as you can. Be fearless, especially if you are typically not very expressive in your face. Stretch, and then fully rest, those muscles.

Activate, release.

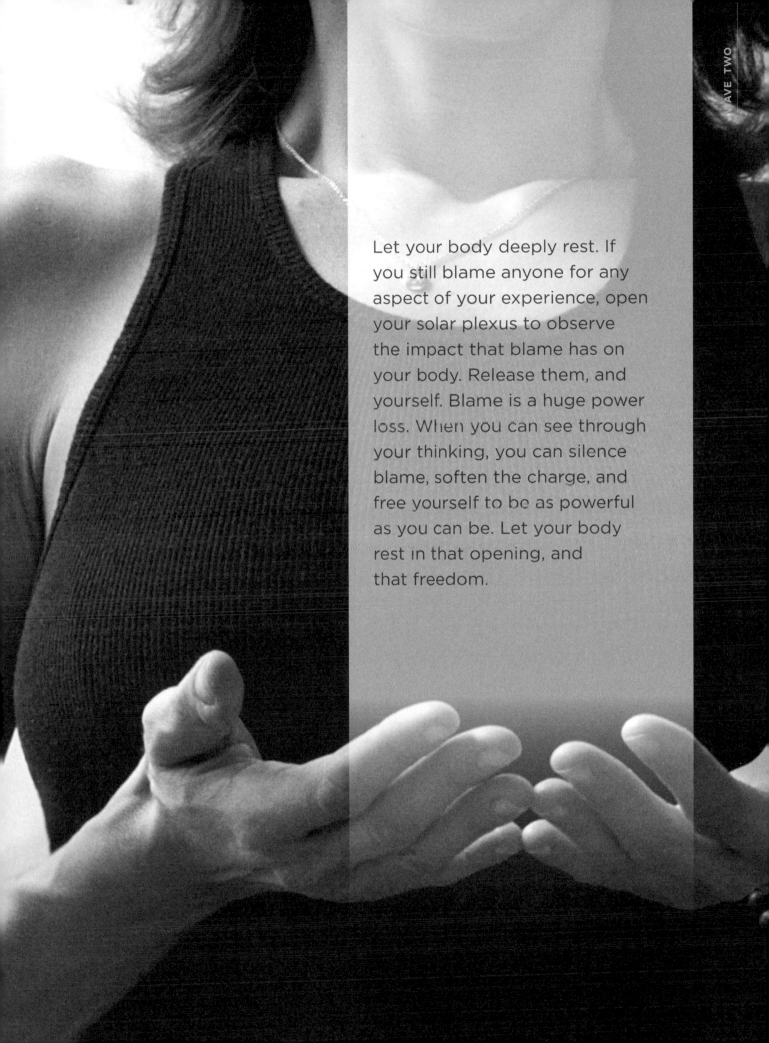

Let your body deeply rest. If you still blame anyone for any aspect of your experience, open your solar plexus to observe the impact that blame has on your body. Release them, and yourself. Blame is a huge power loss. When you can see through your thinking, you can silence blame, soften the charge, and free yourself to be as powerful as you can be. Let your body rest in that opening, and that freedom.

TWIST L/R
knees to one
side, gaze to
the other side

JATHARA PARIVARTANASANA |
SUPINE SPINAL TWIST

Bend your knees to place your feet on the floor.
Bring your knees over to your left for a gentle
twist on the bolster; arms out next to you.

Observe your breathing for a few moments.

Stay on your bolster, bring your knees back to
center, shift your seat just slightly to your left,
then let your knees descend over to your right.

Take at least one more minute

receive this healing opening

OPTION 1
seat on prop

OPTION 2
seat on floor

OPTION 3
fully reclined,
seat on floor

VIRASANA | HERO POSE

Gently bring your feet back to center and slowly rise up to sitting. Keep your bolster where it is. Come on to your hands and knees near the front of your mat for Virasana. Slowly sit back between your feet. If you're new to Virasana, sit on the end of your bolster with your feet on either side (**OPTION 1**). If you'd prefer, sit down in front of your bolster (**OPTION 2**) and slowly lie back in Supta Virasana for a deeper stretch.

Take time to arrange yourself here; root both inner and outer sides down equally and lengthen your tailbone toward your knees. Press the tops of your toes generously down into the floor, and hug your feet with your heels.

You may also remove your bolster and come to a fully reclined posture, breathing deeply (**OPTION 3**). If you're in seated Virasana, rest your hands on your thighs with your palms facing down. Soften the muscles of your face and neck. Root inner and outer thighs down evenly; from your hip sockets, keep your thighs parallel and extend directly out to your knees.

As you sit, breathe into your sides and let those muscles soften and open. Be present for the next few breaths. Root down through the tops of your toes, gently, and breathe into your quadriceps to find more space in your entire body.

One more full minute here. If you are lying down, slowly come to rise up and come towards hands and knees.

OPTION 3
fully reclined,
seat on floor

OPTION 1
seat on prop

Our presence
here shapes
our presence
everywhere.

OPTION 2
seat on floor

*Take several
breaths or several
minutes here.*

TO GAIN MORE CLARITY ON HOW
OUR MEMORY HYPNOTIZES US,
DE SALZMANN WRITES:

*There is in me an essential energy
that is the basis of all that exists.
I don't feel it because my attention is
occupied by everything contained in
my memory, thoughts, images, desires,
disappointments, physical impressions.
I don't know what I am, I don't know
who I can be, yet something tells me to
look and to listen, and to seek seriously
and truly. And when I try to listen, I
see that I am stopped by thoughts and
feelings and I listen poorly, and I'm not
quite enough to hear, to feel; but my
wish to know is more subtle, and I want
the attention that is required to notice.*

HANDS AND KNEES

Leaving the bolster where it is, walk your hands to the front of your mat. Lift up to hands and knees, feel the rush of circulation into your feet, calves, and knees. Slowly lengthen your legs back behind you, toes tucked beneath you.

With your feet on either side of your bolster, slowly make your way back to Downward Facing Dog.

Take five to ten breaths here.

gaze L/R

BALASANA | CHILD'S POSE

From Downward Facing Dog, bring your knees down to the floor. Place your bolster off to the side and let your arms rest in front of you; turn your gaze to the right or let your forehead rest on the floor.

Take this time to bow to those you've been blaming. Bow with gratitude and devotion; they've given you a map to your highest way of seeing. If you've been seeing them through the lens of blame, your work is to stand in front of that perspective and choose another possible view; that is your responsibility and privilege.

Turn your head as needed, and feel this sweet, passive softness, in which you can see clearly, without judgment. It's time to move past the perspective of blame and use this understanding to learn both acceptance and authorship.

Very gently come back to the center and lift your head. Keep your arms out in front of you, bring your bolster to your mat so you can rest your head on it in Downward Facing Dog.

HEAD RESTING ON PROP

SUPPORTED CHILD'S POSE
prop to navel

ADHO MUKHA SHVANASANA |
DOWNWARD FACING DOG

Lift your seat high into Downward Facing Dog
and rest your head on your bolster if possible.
Draw your shoulderblades toward the back of
your heart, then strongly extend from your heart
down through your arms to press into your
palms and fingertips.

Adjust the placement of your head as needed,
to soften your heart more from the inside.

Lower your knees on either side of your bolster,
back down into child's pose; bring your bolster
closer as needed, and rest for several breaths
here. You may turn your head to either side
as needed.

*Slowly come up to sit
on your heels*

and make your way to the
wall for Viparita Karani

PROP UNDER SACRUM
seat against wall

VIPARITA KARANI | LEGS UP THE WALL

Set your bolster up against the wall, scoot your tush up onto the bolster and move your sitting bones as close as possible to the wall. Lengthen your legs up the wall with your seat and sacrum on the bolster; rest your head and shoulders on the floor.

With your legs up the wall, relax your body and hold space for yourself. This is a very healing posture, especially if you spend a lot of time on your feet or in a seat. Let your arms rest at your sides and invite healing, nourishing circulation from your feet into your organs. We are creating the conditions for opening, softening every system in your body (nervous system, lymphatic, circulatory, respiratory, digestive).

Invite healing

relax your hands and all
the muscles of your face

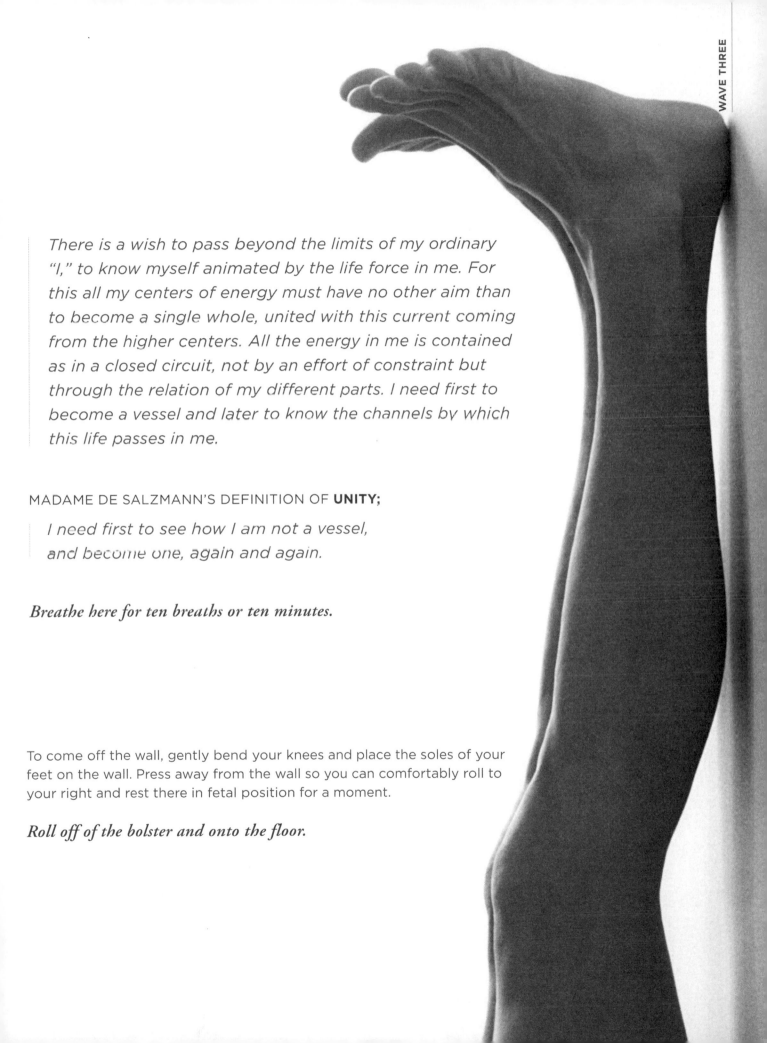

There is a wish to pass beyond the limits of my ordinary "I," to know myself animated by the life force in me. For this all my centers of energy must have no other aim than to become a single whole, united with this current coming from the higher centers. All the energy in me is contained as in a closed circuit, not by an effort of constraint but through the relation of my different parts. I need first to become a vessel and later to know the channels by which this life passes in me.

MADAME DE SALZMANN'S DEFINITION OF **UNITY;**

*I need first to see how I am not a vessel,
and become one, again and again.*

Breathe here for ten breaths or ten minutes.

To come off the wall, gently bend your knees and place the soles of your feet on the wall. Press away from the wall so you can comfortably roll to your right and rest there in fetal position for a moment.

Roll off of the bolster and onto the floor.

OPTION 1
shoulders on
the floor

OPTION 2
sit bones on
the floor

OPTION 3
sit bones on
the floor,
head elevated

SHAVASANA
come to rest

SHAVASANA | CORPSE POSE

Let your body receive
with gratitude and
sweetness

Return to your mat and arrange a bolster, 2 blankets, pillows, towels or a couch cushion beneath your middle back. It should extend down to your mid-thighs, with a block or books to prop up your feet.

Take your time arranging your poses to create the conditions for rest.

For **OPTION 1** the top edge of the bolster should rest right between and just below your shoulderblades, for a nice, passive opening in your heart.

OPTION 1

For **OPTION 2** rest your ankles on your bolster and lie flat on the floor.

> *The sense of my life today is to be entirely available to the presence in me, through a state in which I will be completely passive and yet very awake.*
>
> - MADAME DE SALZMANN

As a result of this practice may we enter into a challenging situation actively listening, entirely awake.

You may choose to stay here or come down for Shavasana.

For **OPTION 3** bring your seat down on the floor and come back into supported Shavasana. You may also choose to place the block/prop under the top of your blankets/bolster/cushion(s), and lie down on that arrangement.

OPTION 1
shoulders on
the floor

OPTION 2
sit bones on
the floor

OPTION 3
sit bones
on the floor,
head elevated

AWAKENING

Stay passive, awake and listening; gently begin to deepen your breathing. Softly bring your feet to the floor with your knees bent. Let your knees touch and take your feet almost as wide as your mat, a little wider than your hips. Take a few very deep, very nourishing breaths. Very gently turn to your right side and take fetal position either on or off your bolster, as you like. Slowly come up to sitting. Rest your hands on your thighs and close your eyes. Take a look at your state now, with your eyes closed.

SNAPSHOT

Take a full impression of your entire being. Quiet, healing, receptive, listening.

Fold your hands in front of your heart in prayer.

To be completely passive - quiet, listening - is really an active state.

Bring your chin to your chest.

To all the ways in which we use this practice as a form of healing, moving ourselves into a unity that reveals within us a current of purity and light.

To all of our teachers, past, present and future, and to your own heart.

NAMASTE.

SANKALPA

THERE IS NOBODY TO

BLAME.

NOTHING TO FEAR.
NOWHERE TO HIDE.
NO SECRET TO KEEP.

THERE IS ONE

LOVE.

ONE LIGHT.
ONE HEART.
ONE BODY.
ONE PRIVILEGE.
ONE SOURCE.
ONE FAMILY.

OBSERVE RATHER THAN FIX.

TRY TO
RIZE
WN.

THE SOURCE OF OUR INSPIRATION
IS FROM A PLACE WHERE THERE IS
NO RELIGION, ONLY TRUTH.

- RODNEY COLLIN

TALKING POINTS

SO LET US STOP ENTIRELY BLAMING OTHERS
FOR A BAD WORLD. LET US BEGIN TO
RECOGNIZE THAT THIS BAD WORLD EXISTS,
PRIMARILY, ONLY IN OUR OWN CRANIUM;
THAT OUTSIDE WE ACTUALLY LIVE IN A
UNIVERSE UNFOLDING IN JUSTICE, A PLACE
IN WHICH HUMAN SOULS AND OTHER FORMS
OF LIFE ARE LEARNING BY EXPERIENCE
TO LIVE WELL.

-MANLY HALL

QUIET, HEALING, RECEPTIVE, LISTENING

AIM: _____

WAVE ONE

WAVE TWO

WAVE THREE

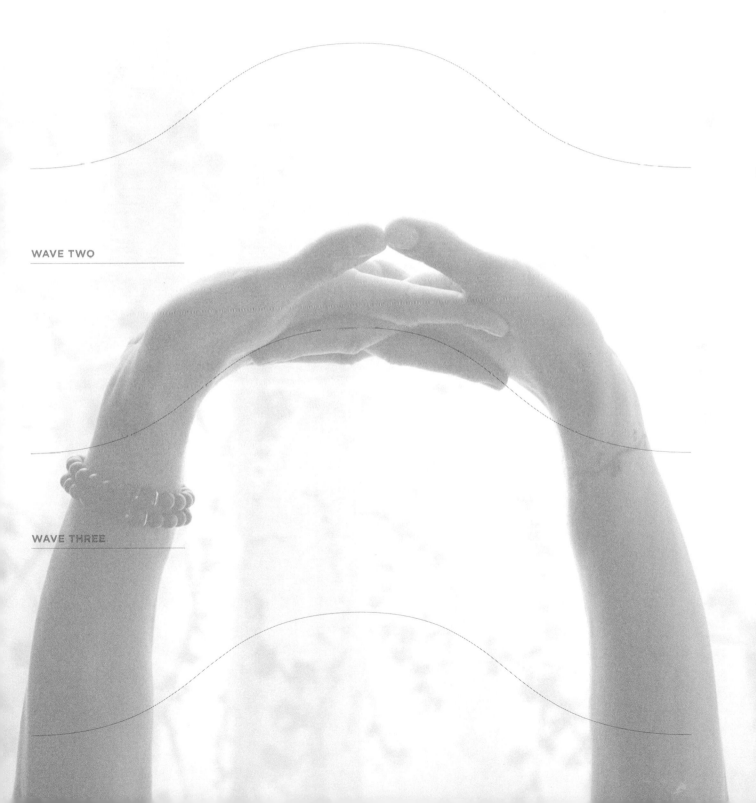

AWAKENING

DEFINITION OF
UNITY:

I NEED FIRST TO SEE HOW
I AM NOT A VESSEL, AND BECOME ONE,
AGAIN AND AGAIN.

- MADAME DE SALZMANN

DONNA KARAN

BREATHE AND FIND STILLNESS. HOW SIMPLE AND DEEPLY COMPLEX THIS IS! We live in a modern world with constant movement and a multiplicity of multitasking.

My life really is DKNY – I am constantly in the hustle and bustle of New York, a city that has been both an endless source of inspiration and a constant challenge for me. The city is electric, magnetic and constantly in motion. I love it. But, even still, I desire to find that stillness, to center through breath, to create a calm within the chaos. For me, it's yoga. I started practicing yoga when I was an 18-year-old girl and I've been in love with it ever since. Yoga is how I first learned to find the calm within in the chaos; a concept that has now become a philosophy of living I embrace through my foundation, center and retail collection, Urban Zen.

I think that the beauty of Yoga is that it allows you to drop the ego of the "me" so you can think about the "we." This is something that Elena has been able to achieve through her teaching.

My connection with Elena has been on many levels. She is a woman who embodies Urban Zen, from guiding thousands of yoga students on the Great Lawn in Central Park to leading deeply soulful classes at the Urban Zen Center, to joining me for personal healing and grounding at Parrot Cay.

The beauty of Yoga is that it allows you to drop the ego of the "me" so you can think about the "we."

My dream for Parrot Cay is to see it used as place and space where people come together to find that calm that we're all seeking; a place to be still, to breathe. I love that Elena has embraced Parrot Cay in this way. Parrot Cay is where I reconnect with my loved ones and, truly, where I reconnect with myself.

Connection is what it's all about and it is conscious breath that allows us go within, refocus and feel connected once again.

So, yes, be still, breathe and find the calm within the chaos.

YOU ARE INVITED TO RECONNECT TO YOURSELF THROUGH STILLNESS.

CHAPTER THREE

BREATHE AND FIND STILLNESS

photography by **ALICE MARSHALL** *mandala artwork by* **SOFIA ESCOBAR**

Certain aspects of ourselves that seem like immutable, profound tendencies are actually just impulses, residues we carry, not actually "us."

Yoga helps us see and reframe it all.

SANKALPA

WELCOME TO YOUR PRACTICE TODAY.

This efficient and effective breathing and meditation practice is for you whether you've had years of experience meditating - or no experience at all.

With this practice, we learn how to simply observe.

Turn your palms to face down on your thighs and bring your upper arms to rest alongside your upper body. Close and soften your eyes; turn your attention inside.

MY OBSERVATION

The impulse and inspiration for this practice: *May we practice being more present for ourselves.* Why do we run away when we're scared of something? Why do we keep ourselves busy with work, dishes, cleaning, organizing? Some of us get lazy or complacent, others of us have specific escapes like drugs, damaging situations, destructive people or distracting tasks. How can we use our practices of meditation and breathing to be there for ourselves, no matter how dire or scary the circumstances? In the same way that we are there for our most revered friends, can we use this practice to be truly present for ourselves?

Notice the weight of your hands resting on your thighs.
Take a few minutes to breathe deeply here.

OBSERVE

Begin to observe where your breathing feels blocked and where it moves freely.

Invite your breathing into every peripheral point in your body. As you observe, notice any aspects of your experience - such as fear, sadness, or doubt - that seem to be immutable, unchangeable presences in your body.

As we explore these aspects that seem ingrained, we begin to learn that they are just residues, outworn coping mechanisms we've adopted during our lives. Such tendencies are not here to stay. May we use this practice to see and shift them.

Any reactivity we observe is indicative of the impulses, or states of being, as they pass through us.

As you breathe, you may notice your mind formulating thoughts such as, *"I'm angry, I'm sad, I'm terrified,"* in which case you've named your whole being with the label of this passing state. This practice of noticing asks us to see differently. *"Aha! I'm seeing anger passing through my body right now; I'm seeing terror passing through my body right now."*

This meditation nourishes and oxygenates our bodies, which helps us to watch these states, like weather patterns, passing through.

anger

terror

sadness

SADNESS

ANGER

TERROR

Keep your hands resting with your palms facing down. Watch those little impulses, residues, coping mechanisms, states of being; hold a sense of humor and love for all of your observations.

Breathe as deeply as you can. When you notice something challenging coming up (and It always will), make your breathing bigger and more resonant, throughout your body.

UJJAYI BREATHING

HAAAA

HAAAA

First, inhale and exhale while making a "haaaaa" sound, with your mouth slightly open.

Inhale. Exhale.

Let the breath resonate in the back of your throat rather than in your nostrils, for the next two minutes. This is called Ujjayi breathing; victoriously uprising breath. Notice how your breathing helps you see and make space between one thought and the next. *May our practice help us see clearly to reframe negativity and choose responses that are helpful and uplifting.*

HAAAA

 HAAAA

Now, make the same "haaaaa" sound with your mouth closed.

Feel that resonance throughout your throat, and upward into your eyes.

SOLAR PLEXUS

To locate your solar plexus, follow your bottom ribs with your fingers - from your waist to the center of your chest, where your bottom ribs meet. Rest your left hand there, on your solar plexus, at first; keep your right hand on your right thigh for now.

ASK: *How can I be there for myself? Why is it that I can be so present for my friends and people I love and not for myself?*

With this practice, breathe and connect to this source of power in your body. Keep your hand there, lean back into your seat and breathe this space open.

ASK: *When a thought comes, does this central space in my body close or open in conjunction with that thought? If the space closes with a certain thought, there is more room to grow and expand that space. When we make more space physiologically and architecturally in the body,*

we have a larger backdrop on which to dissipate and dissolve doubtful trains of thought.

Place your right hand on top of your left.

ANYTIME - in a pose, seated, standing, in a conversation or interaction - place your hands in this way and open that space with confidence, clarity and power. This central point is a source of power and presence.

NOTE: This power isn't power *over* anyone. We're cultivating power to be present for *ourselves.* Everyone near us benefits from that quality of presence. Keep breathing here for a few more breaths.

Release your hands down onto your sides and turn your palms up.

As we breathe, we are demystifying, breaking down what we perceive to be overcoming us, overtaking us.

Moods, states, impulses - we are breaking these down into energy, knowable parts, seeing them like weather patterns, like clouds, passing through us at any given time.

We are *seeing* that central point of *stillness.*

We arc giving ourselves the opportunity to author appropriate responses to each situation that arises.

May we learn to allow the stillness in our hearts to live in our minds.

Keep your palms facing up and breathe into your solar plexus. Now, focus on filling the back and sides of that space with your breathing.

Ten more breaths here.

Notice the baseline of
softness and openness
always present

JNANA MUDRA

Bring your index fingers and thumbs to touch in Jnana Mudra, the seal of wisdom. With this mudra, we seal and absorb the wisdom of our practice into our being. This sweet sitting practice will impact all we do.

When you feel reactive, this practice brings **PAUSE**.

When you feel rushed, this practice brings **STILLNESS**.

When you feel closed, this practice brings **OPENING**.

AWAKENING

Fold your hands in front of your heart in prayer. Continue to breathe deeply and bring awareness to each breath as it arrives and is gently released.

Any time you are feeling doubtful, disconnected or numb, *sit down for this practice.* Take a few breaths and watch. Place your attention on the space of your solar plexus, and place your hands there gently. *Feel* this power center and fill your interior space with the most attentive, loving nourishment.

May we connect to this space and shift toward healing.

Bring your chin into your chest.

To the respectful and complete healing of your body, your mind and your heart, we bow.

NAMASTE.

SANKALPA

THE CORE OF YOGA PRACTICE WORKS
WITH WHAT'S ALREADY PRESENT
TO IDENTIFY OBSTRUCTIONS TO
THE BREATHING AND THE FUNCTION
OF THE MIND.

- LESLIE KAMINOFF

WE ARE NOT CHANGING WHAT HAPPENED -
WE ARE CHANGING THE WAY IT LIVES IN US.

AWAKENING

WHAT I NEED FOR
HEALING IS ALREADY
PRESENT IN MY SYSTEM.

- LESLIE KAMINOFF

GWYNETH PALTROW

WHAT IS IT TO EXPLORE OUR HIGHEST POSSIBILITIES? In many ways this concept has become the thesis for my life. It's a question I ask myself everyday. How can I truly realize my potential? What is my potential? Who defines it? Is it society's idea of what I am meant to achieve, or is it more difficult to understand? Is it a set of goals that my ego has constructed to cement my idea of value to myself and the outside world? Or is it perhaps a deeper calling?

In my experience, my highest possibilities have always lived behind doors I'd refused to open because I was afraid to confront or disappoint. It is only when I have opened those doors that I have seen the possibilities behind them. Where there was perceived confrontation, I've found authenticity, and when I was afraid of not pleasing others, I found my truth.

For many years, I strived to achieve what I thought was my highest possibility. I tried to be the best career woman, mother, friend. I went into other areas of work with a kind of fearlessness that I didn't even understand. What was I doing? Was I trying to prove something to myself, or was I trying to emerge? I was trying to achieve my potential in those areas, I still am. However, the external world never seems to hold the answer, the way I hold it in my consciousness. And while it doesn't always look the way I'd expected, it is only when I begin to uncover my own truth that I am my best.

> *Was I trying to prove something to myself,* or was I trying to emerge?

"To thine own self be true," said Shakespeare. And this is not a platitude. For me, it is the key to life. It is the springboard for discovering what IS possible. It is what we are all on Earth for. It is the real task that the universe sets forth for us; to stretch through the very idea of what we may be realizing for ourselves, to the higher ideal of what we can become.

How can I truly realize my potential?

This chapter provides us with a moment to explore those possibilities. Yoga always provides us the opportunity to go deeper, to tune in. Through Elena and Erica's beautiful approach to physical openness and mindfulness, we can begin to uncover where our own possibilities might lie.

YOU ARE INVITED TO BE OF SERVICE TO YOURSELF AND TO OTHERS.

CHAPTER FOUR

EXPLORE YOUR HIGHEST POSSIBILITIES

photography by **MICHAEL CHICHI** *and* **DOMINIC NEITZ**
portals by **HARLAN EMIL**

YOUR CHOICE: Be an unconscious slave to your habitual tendencies, or be a conscious servant to your highest possibilities. Locate and revel in the vast space within, and in all the ways in which you can open your habitual tensions, listen better and heal your reactivity in order to *serve* in your life. This Level 2/3 sequence refines your shoulder alignment through a thoughtful standing sequence, seated hip openers, arm balances and backbends.

While a tyrant wants power over others, a true magician desires power over only himself. Being an unconscious slave, we often seek to control unconsciously; being a conscious servant, we are here to serve, to help, to uplift, to provide.

SANKALPA

Welcome. Take a nice comfortable seat.
Rest your hands with your palms facing down.

THE POTENT QUESTION:

**ARE YOU GOING TO BE AN UNCONSCIOUS SLAVE
OR A CONSCIOUS SERVANT?**

Far from being bound in a negative way, being in
service is actually a great gift we can give. We have
the capacity to serve anyone or anything in our lives.

Fold your hands in front of your heart.

With this practice, you'll work methodically and logically through a series of sweet arm balances to learn how to serve and nourish your own heart.

SHOULDER ALIGNMENT

1 Inhale with presence to lengthen the sides of your waist upward.

2 Fearlessly move the heads of your arm bones back.

3 Bring the tips of your shoulderblades toward the back of your heart.

4 Turn forearm muscles in and upper arm muscles out to expand your collarbones.

5 Expand everything consciously from that integrated architecture.

And in the space of that integrated,
beautiful container, expand this vessel
of light as you breathe.
Choose to be a conscious servant,
aligned, intentional and clear.

Inhale deeply.

Bow to yourself.
May we explore being conscious servants
to our highest possibilities.

Gently release your hands.

EXPLORE YOUR HIGHEST POSSIBILITIES

SHOULDER ALIGNMENT

1 Lengthen both sides of your body long.

2 Bring the heads of your arm bones back.

3 Gently press the bottom tips of your shoulderblades into the back of your heart.

4 Energetically turn your forearms in and your upper arms out.

5 Expand that entire form from the inside out.

WAVE ONE

SUN SALUTATIONS AND
HEART-OPENING TWISTS

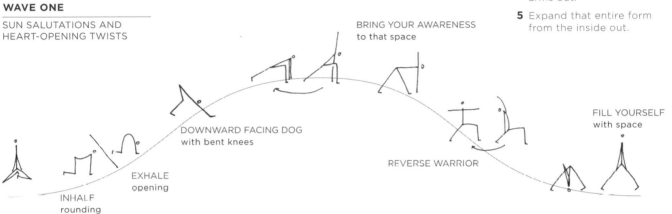

BRING YOUR AWARENESS
to that space

DOWNWARD FACING DOG
with bent knees

FILL YOURSELF
with space

EXHALE
opening

REVERSE WARRIOR

INHALE
rounding

WAVE TWO

INVERSIONS, SEATED HIP
OPENERS AND TWISTS

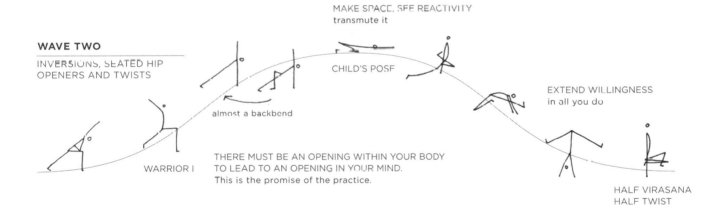

MAKE SPACE, SEE REACTIVITY
transmute it

CHILD'S POSE

EXTEND WILLINGNESS
in all you do

almost a backbend

WARRIOR I

THERE MUST BE AN OPENING WITHIN YOUR BODY
TO LEAD TO AN OPENING IN YOUR MIND.
This is the promise of the practice.

HALF VIRASANA
HALF TWIST

WAVE THREE

ARM BALANCES AND
SPINE OPENERS

ANY SITUATION
hold it in front of you

SERVING
your family,
friends, work

IF WE HAVE A LONGING FOR THE TRUTH,
THE MOMENT WE SEE IT,
we have a longing to serve it.

Inhale rounding

exhale opening

PULSATION

CAT/COW TO DOWNWARD FACING DOG WITH BENT KNEES

Come onto your hands and knees; inhale to round your spine. Exhale to open and extend it. On the exhalation, lengthen the sides of your waist. One more time, big breath in, round your spine. This time stay there as you exhale, and draw your lower belly up and in. Now inhale and lengthen from your waist all the way up under your arms to open yourself up, face up, soft, relaxed gaze.

Tuck your toes, reach back, Downward Facing Dog.

As you breathe in Downward Facing Dog, bend your knees deeply and reach your sitting bones high to the sky. Then root your thighbones back and draw energy up from your hands, up your arms, into the back of your heart. From your heart, root back down through your hands, extend your fingers, your fingernails. **EXTEND.**

Extend willingness
in all you do

PARIVRITTA ANJANEYASANA
HIGH LUNGE TWIST

Place your right foot between your hands; reach
your right arm high to the sky for your twist.
Stretch the sides of your waist long; with each
inhalation lengthen from your waist upward. With
each exhalation draw your upper arm bones back
in space; bring your heart back, head back.

*Right hand down; step back to
Downward Facing Dog. Keep the
sides of your body long.*

SECOND SIDE: Place your left foot outside your
left hand; left arm high. This opening in
your body makes room for a potent shift in
your mind. To open space: bring the heads
of your arm bones back; bottom tips of
shoulderblades towards the back of your
heart; turn your forearms in and your upper
arms out. Then expand that shape; make
everything spacious.

The willingness to shift perspective,
to hold dexterity of perspective,
comes from within your body.
There must be an opening
within your body to lead to
an opening in your mind.
This is the promise of
the practice.

Make room interiorly
for your breathing

UTTHITA TRIKONASANA
TRIANGLE

Right foot between your hands, left heel to the floor. Reach your innermost sitting bones back behind you, left hand to left waist. Lengthen the sides of your body long. Heads of your arm bones back, press the bottom tips of your shoulderblades towards the back of your heart. Bring your outer thighs back, send your tailbone down, left arm high to the sky. From your hips expand and lengthen in every direction.

Breathe five to ten breaths, then place your left hand down to the floor, Plank Pose, Chaturanga Dandasana, Upward Facing Dog. Exhale back Downward Facing Dog.

Any situation, any aggravation you're currently managing - hold it right in front of you. *Are you going to be a slave to that sensation? Or will you be a conscious servant to healing within that context?*

YOUR CHOICE:
Be a slave to every passing sensation in your body, or serve the situation optimally.

About every 1.5 seconds we have a different thought or feeling. *Can we make enough space to see passing situations and sensations as they enter and exit this body? And within that space, can we choose how we respond in a healing way?*

Left foot between your hands, Trikonasana.

Left hand to the floor, right hand to your waist. Ground through your feet, draw your feet towards one another, widen your seat, make space throughout your pelvis. Then lengthen the sides of your body long to create space in your upper body. Heads of the arm bones back, draw the bottom tips of your shoulderblades in towards your heart. Turn forearms in energetically, upper arms out energetically. Lengthen your tailbone long beneath you, tuck your left seat strongly beneath you. Now EXPAND that perfectly integrated shape. Once you've made all this space, can you see clearly through your reactions to what most aggravates you? Rather than being a slave to this passing situation, can you make more space to serve the truth instead?

Step back to Plank Pose, Chaturanga Dandasana, Upward Facing Dog, Downward Facing Dog.

VIRABHADRASANA II | WARRIOR II TO
VIPARITA VIRABHADRASANA
REVERSE WARRIOR

Step your right foot between your hands for Warrior II. Keep both lungs full, lengthen the sides of your body long, heads of the arm bones back, bottom tips of the shoulderblades in. Turn forearms in, upper arms out; expand that entire shape in all directions.

Bring your back hand to your back leg for Reverse Warrior. Reach the heads of both arm bones back; breathe more space into your heart. Whatever your typical reactions, through your practice, you can imprint upon your body a different, more healing response.

Inhale deeply into your left lung. Exhale both hands down to the floor; Chaturanga Dandasana, inhale Upward Facing Dog, exhale Downward Facing Dog.

Left foot between hands, Warrior II. Lengthen sides of your body long, integrate your shoulders onto your back. Make space within; bring your back arm to your back leg. The space we make internally helps us see where we are an unconscious slave, sleeping and reacting - and in that space we can devise another strategy - more consciously SERVING.

Back to Downward Facing Dog.

Heal reactivity in your body
practice the act of responding elegantly

SERVING

To serve our friends,
our families,
our profession,
is a privilege.
Let this understanding
be truly reflected in
your behavior.

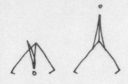

PRASARITA PADOTTANASANA
WIDE-LEGGED FORWARD BEND WITH
HANDS INTERLACED **TO**
TADASANA | MOUNTAIN POSE

Step your left foot forward; turn both
feet to face the right side of your mat.
Walk your hands to the center of your
mat, clasp your hands behind your
back and reach them up and over your
head. Lengthen the sides of your waist
long, draw the heads of your arm bones
back, and bring the bottom tips of your
shoulderblades towards the back of your
heart. With that integration, turn your
forearms in towards one another, upper
arm bones out away from one another.
Breathe fully, and feel the internal and
structural openings in your body.

*Bend your elbows gently,
send your thighbones back,
inhale up to stand.*

With your hands interlaced behind your back, stand tall and feel the space in the sides of your heart. Every time you bring your awareness to that space, you shift away from reactivity.

Too often we end our yoga practice
and lose our spaciousness.
Specifically notice that contraction.
This is what's known as
"remembering yourself."

UTTHITA PARSVAKONASANA
SIDE ANGLE

Turn your right foot forward, left heel back, bend your front knee deeply. Right forearm to your front thigh, left arm up and long over your ear. Make space in your body to allow yourself to see whatever your reactivity is, and transmute it. From slave to servant, sleeping to awake.

Turn to face the left side now, right heel back, left forearm to your left thigh, right arm up over your ear. Powerfully plant both feet on the floor and make more space in your body to accurately see where you've been draining your energy by being a slave to some opinion or assumption. Then shift the momentum you observe in your reactivity into your service.

Place your hands on the floor. Inhale to Plank Pose, exhale Chaturanga Dandasana; inhale Upward Facing Dog, exhale Downward Facing Dog.

Make space, see reactivity

transmute it

VIRABHADRASANA I
WARRIOR I

Step your right foot forward, bend your front knee deeply. *See yourself.* Lengthen from your waist upward, draw your upper arm bones back and bring your shoulderblades toward the back of your heart. Turn your forearms in, upper arms out. Expand that space circumferentially and be awake for yourself.

Place your hands on the floor. Inhale to Plank Pose, exhale Chaturanga Dandasana; inhale Upward Facing Dog, exhale Downward Facing Dog.

Step your left foot between your hands for Warrior I, arms high. Take this time to practice watching reactivity in your mind and body. Seeing our almost-reaction, and then shifting away from it - that is our privilege. Bend your front knee deeply. Fill up with so much awareness, light, and time - and lean into it, so everyone near you can feel both your effort and your elegance.

Inhale back Plank Pose, exhale Chaturanga, inhale Upward Facing Dog, exhale Downward Facing Dog.

Seeing our almost-reaction,
and then shifting away from it
that is our privilege

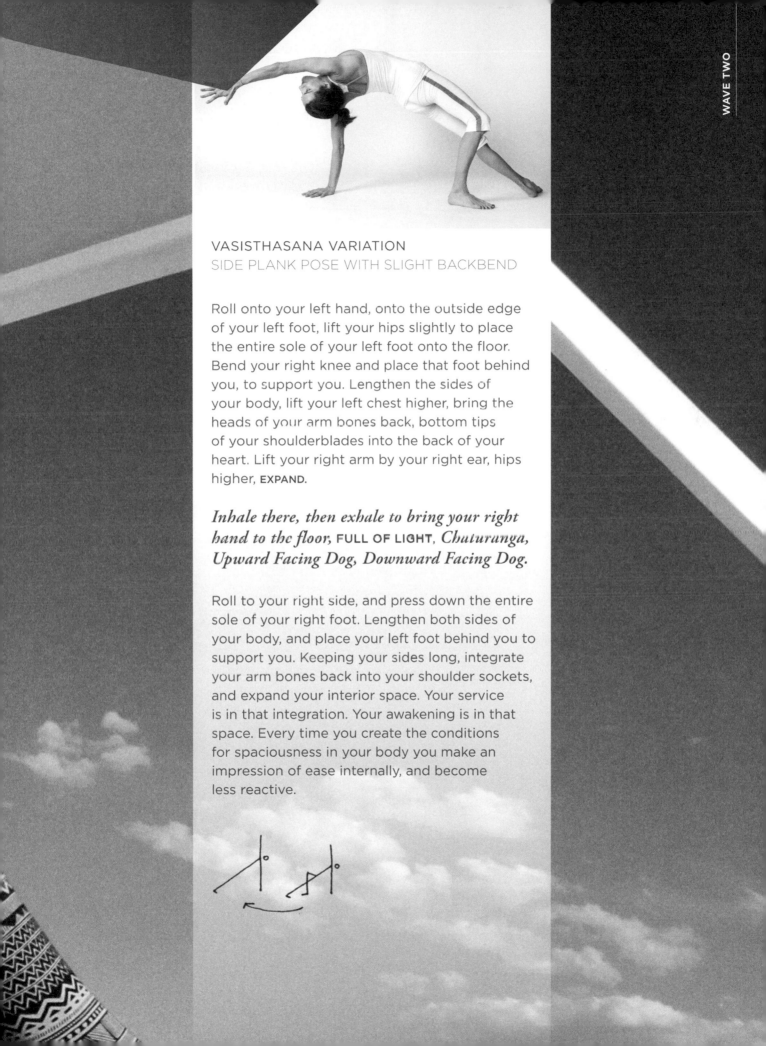

VASISTHASANA VARIATION
SIDE PLANK POSE WITH SLIGHT BACKBEND

Roll onto your left hand, onto the outside edge
of your left foot, lift your hips slightly to place
the entire sole of your left foot onto the floor.
Bend your right knee and place that foot behind
you, to support you. Lengthen the sides of
your body, lift your left chest higher, bring the
heads of your arm bones back, bottom tips
of your shoulderblades into the back of your
heart. Lift your right arm by your right ear, hips
higher, **EXPAND.**

*Inhale there, then exhale to bring your right
hand to the floor,* **FULL OF LIGHT,** *Chaturanga,
Upward Facing Dog, Downward Facing Dog.*

Roll to your right side, and press down the entire
sole of your right foot. Lengthen both sides of
your body, and place your left foot behind you to
support you. Keeping your sides long, integrate
your arm bones back into your shoulder sockets,
and expand your interior space. Your service
is in that integration. Your awakening is in that
space. Every time you create the conditions
for spaciousness in your body you make an
impression of ease internally, and become
less reactive.

BALASANA | CHILD'S POSE

Reach your seat back onto your heels. Hold the soles of your feet with your hands to complete the circuit of connection to yourself. Breathe deeply. We are lucky to have this practice, this opportunity to watch ourselves, and learn how we can see and evolve what lives in us, both as our lineage and as our choice.

We must heal ourselves, our families and the world by addressing ourselves and our practice in a healing way.

Here we bow to our
teachers and our families.

Can you make
more space?

Can you breathe another breath
in the service of your own heart?

EKA PADA RAJAKAPOTASANA
ONE-LEGGED KING PIGEON POSE

Bring your right knee forward between your hands for Pigeon. Come down onto your elbows, hands in prayer on the floor in front of you. Sides of your body long, heads of your arm bones back, press your shoulderblades in and buoyantly move your heart forward toward your hands. Turn your forearms in so your thumbs press more strongly and inner arms root down. Turn your upper arm bones back - *feel your interior space; expand within the confines of this architecture, this shape.* Breathe space around every organ and notice what kind of tension and contraction you habitually maintain.

Breathe five breaths to several minutes here.

Left knee forward; come down onto your elbows once again, hands in prayer. For exploration's sake, walk your elbows closer to you - shorten the sides of your waist. Maintain that architecturally. Internally, lengthen from your waist to your armpits, hug your forearms towards one another, roll your upper arm bones away from one another, and then expand the space. See what's possible; even when you are confined structurally, you can make enough space to see every single reaction before it manifests as a word or a movement. Now walk your hands forward to lengthen and relax in that space.

Hold that space for a few minutes.

JANU SIRSASANA
HEAD-TO-KNEE FORWARD BEND

Swing your right leg around for Janu Sirsasana. Bring your arms on either side of your right leg; root both sitting bones down into the ground. With your left heel in your left inner groin, walk your hands out over your right leg, just as far as you can. Root your right thighbone down strongly, draw those baby toes toward you, and from that grounding, inhale the sides of your body long; exhale to pause. Bring the heads of your arm bones back, move the bottom tips of your shoulderblades toward your heart, walk your hands out a bit farther. Feel the difference in your two sides. The commitment we make to service depends deeply on how we ground ourselves. **EXPERIMENT:** Let your right leg go slack. Feel how the entire enterprise falls apart, then reground for one full breath.

Slowly come back up, rest your hands on your thighs and sit tall for a few breaths, with eyes closed, to feel the delicious space in your body. Switch legs.

SECOND SIDE: Place your right heel against your right inner groin. Walk your hands out on either side of your left leg. Lengthen both sides of your waist evenly. Can you make the conscious choice to create the space that is needed? **LISTEN.** Notice where in your body or mind you are enslaved, and shift that immediately. Make the choice to serve that which is most beneficial and useful.

Stay for three breaths; long sides, soft heart. Slowly come back up.

UPAVISTHA KONASANA
WIDE-LEGGED SEATED FORWARD BEND

Open both legs wide, and root your inner and outer thighbones down evenly. If your lower back is rounding, prop yourself up on a blanket or rolled-up mat, and root down well. Flex your feet to stabilize. Consciously serve yourself by making space in your own being; in this way you serve everyone close to you. In making this kind of space and ease, you become the most stabilizing force in any situation.

Breathe several breaths or minutes in the pose. Keeping your side body long, slowly sit tall. Take a moment there, hands resting on thighs, palms facing down. Reground and breathe.

Make the conscious choice
become a stabilizing force

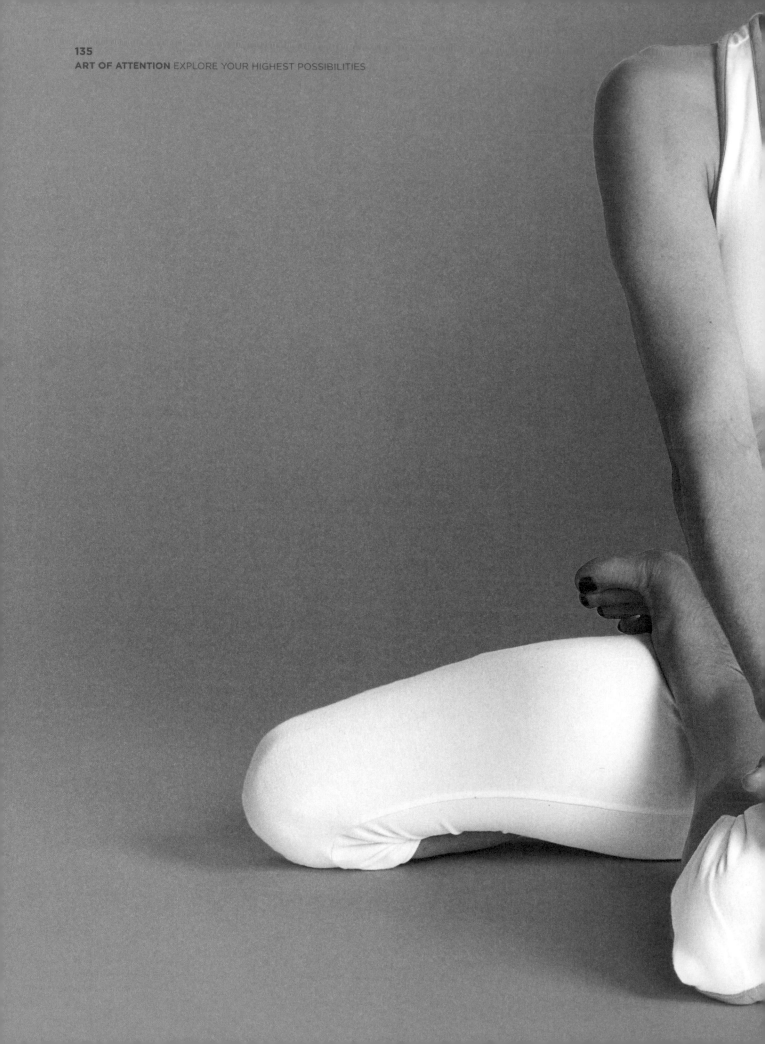

BHARADVAJASANA II
HALF SEATED TWIST

Bring your legs together. Take Ardha Virasana with your right leg; place your outer left foot on your upper right thigh for Bharadvajasana. Take a moment to press both hands into the floor behind you and lift your heart, sides of your body long, heads of your arm bones back, forearms turn in, upper arm bones turn out energetically. To twist, bring your right hand to your left knee, lift long on both sides symmetrically, breathe fully for a few breaths. Come back to center, place your hands face down on your thighs; take a moment to rest and let everything settle back down. This is a good preparatory lengthening pose for your upcoming arm balance.

Breathe a few long breaths here. Keep that length, and come back to the center. Rest here for a moment. Switch sides.

Take Ardha Virasana with your left leg, place your outer right foot on your upper left thigh and root your inner and outer thighs down. Lengthen both sides of your body long. Sense which lung is receiving more breath, and breathe more symmetry into your inner body with your arm bones back. To twist, bring your left hand to your right knee, and lift long on both sides of your waist. Shoulderblades toward your heart to create a strong container for your space interior. *Center yourself and expand interiorly.* That interior space yields ease in the body.

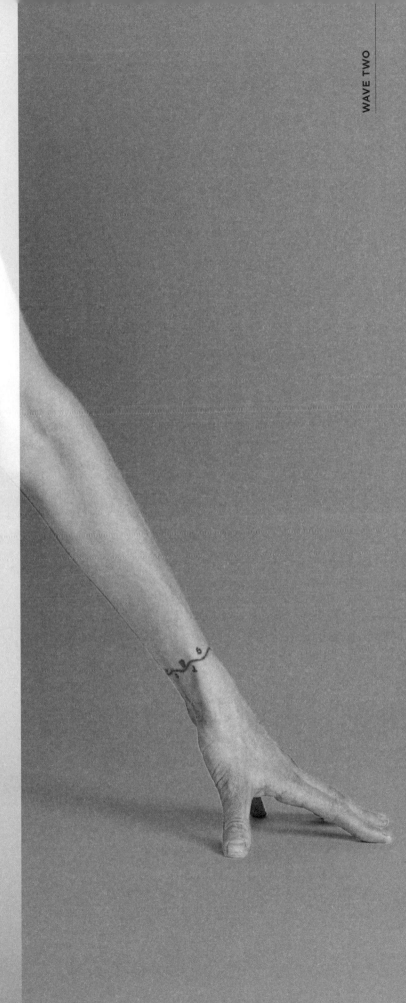

PARSVA BAKASANA / DVI PADA KOUNDINYASANA
SIDE CROW POSE BREAKDOWN

Come to a squat in the middle of your mat, feet together, heels up off the floor. Fold your hands in prayer. Lower your knees down just a bit, lift your heart up internally (I). If you feel yourself wavering, lengthen your breathing - notice more steadiness and spaciousness within yourself. Lean over to your left side, place your left hand on the floor next to you and bring your right arm over your right ear, keep your knees facing forward and lengthen both sides of your body with your breathing (II). Bring the heads of your arm bones back, bottom tips of your shoulderblades in and up, turn your forearms in, upper arms out, and then expand it all. Keep that length and bring your right hand outside your left thigh to the floor about a foot away from your feet, in line with your baby toes. Move your left hand shoulder-width apart from your right.

Smile.

Feel where your left knee is touching your upper right arm (III). Bring your left knee up high onto your upper right arm.

Smile again.

Bend your elbows into Chaturanga arms, and scoot your feet over to the right a bit (IV). Stay spacious interiorly, keep your legs together, flex and lift your feet (V), into Dvi Pada Koundinyasana (VI).

Take a few breaths there and return to your Standing Forward Bend.

IV   V   VI

Smile

shift into spaciousness

Take your squat once again (I). Knees touching, feet touching, breathe the space of your heart open. Bring your right hand to the floor next to you, lengthen your left arm alongside your left ear; breathe both sides of your waist long and expand your interior space (II). Keep that space and turn to your right; extend your left arm over your right thigh, place the hand about a foot away from your feet. Move your right hand about a shoulder-width apart from your left (III). Lift your right knee high up onto your upper left arm, walk your feet out to your left little by little to lift them (V). Flex both feet and lengthen both legs up and out to the side into the pose (VI). **HEART FORWARD.**

Take a few breaths there and come to sitting.

SIDDHASANA / SUKHASANA
SEATED

Center yourself. Place your hands behind you to open your heart. For Siddhasana line up your heels in front of your pelvic floor. For Sukhasana take a comfortable cross-legged seat.

Lift the back of your heart and breathe spaciously.

SETU BANDHASANA TO URDHVA DHANURASANA | BRIDGE TO FULL WHEEL

Keeping that space in your upper body, lie down on your back and bend your knees, feet flat to the floor. For Bridge pose, Setu Bandhasana, press down into your elbows to lift the back and sides of your heart. Stand well on your feet, lengthen the sides of your body long, press the heads of your arm bones back, and the bottom tips of your shoulderblades in toward your heart. Breathe space in, consciously serving your body, your organs, your systems, and the communication between your systems. *We consciously serve everyone around us by creating and holding this space within ourselves.*

Maintaining this opening, place your hands by your ears; press down to rise up to full wheel. Keep the sides of your body long, root your feet, bring the heads of your arm bones back, bottom tips of your shoulderblades in toward your heart.

Expand from the center of your body in every direction for a few breaths, and then slowly lower down.

CAVEAT: Let this ancient teaching simmer awhile; see where you are, in your own life, an unconscious slave, before you judge anyone else. Try not to teach everybody around you how enslaved they are. It's a privilege to see ourselves clearly and free *ourselves* from this prison. If we have a longing for the truth, the moment we see it, we have a longing to serve it.

SECOND TIME: Place your hands for full wheel: super strong feet, shoulderblades towards the back of your heart, lengthen your legs, and expand from the back of your heart down to your feet.

For three to five breaths, lengthen your legs even more, in service. When you're ready, look up to lower down.

JATHARA PARIVARTANASANA | SUPINE SPINAL TWIST

Let both knees fall over to your left side first. Breathe into your interior space for a few breaths. Bring your knees back to the center, then over to your right side. *May we hold this space within ourselves to transition from unconscious slave to conscious servant.*

Come back to the center. Bring your knees into your chest and hug them in.

RE-ROOT THIGHS

Lengthen both legs high to the sky, feet softly flexed. Bring your hands to the back of your hamstrings and ground your shoulderblades into the floor. As you are spreading the hamstring muscles from your inner legs outward, press your thighbones into the windows of your hamstrings there, for at least 5 breaths, stretching the balls of your feet towards the sky.

Gently release both legs to the floor, extend them down and take Shavasana.

SHAVASANA | CORPSE

Corpse, rest.

AWAKENING

Begin to deepen your breathing; stretch your body long. Draw your knees into your chest slowly and roll to your right side. Take a few breaths there in fetal position to gently bring your awareness back. Slowly come up to sitting, close your eyes, and let your hands rest on your thighs, palms down.

There is a dynamism, a spontaneous virtuosity we can cultivate, over time, with care and consistency. *A virtuosity of responsiveness,* with whatever is presented; consistently responding in a way that serves the highest good. If each of us uses this particular practice to choose responsiveness, we will inspire countless fellow humans to take better care of themselves and our planet.

Fold your hands in front of your heart.

We are practicing being watchful of the ways in which we are enslaved to outworn beliefs, assumptions and opinions. And there must be a longing, a deep need to break down these tensions in our body, so that we can really be present and awake rather than enslaved to our habits and tendencies. Spaciously we serve the highest good.

NAMASTE

May our practice bring us to a place
of conscious, sweet servitude of the highest order.
To all of our teachers, who teach us to serve and explore
our highest possibilities, we bow.

SANKALPA

TO BE A LIGHT TO
ONESELF IS THE LIGHT
OF ALL OTHERS.

- J. KRISHNAMURTI

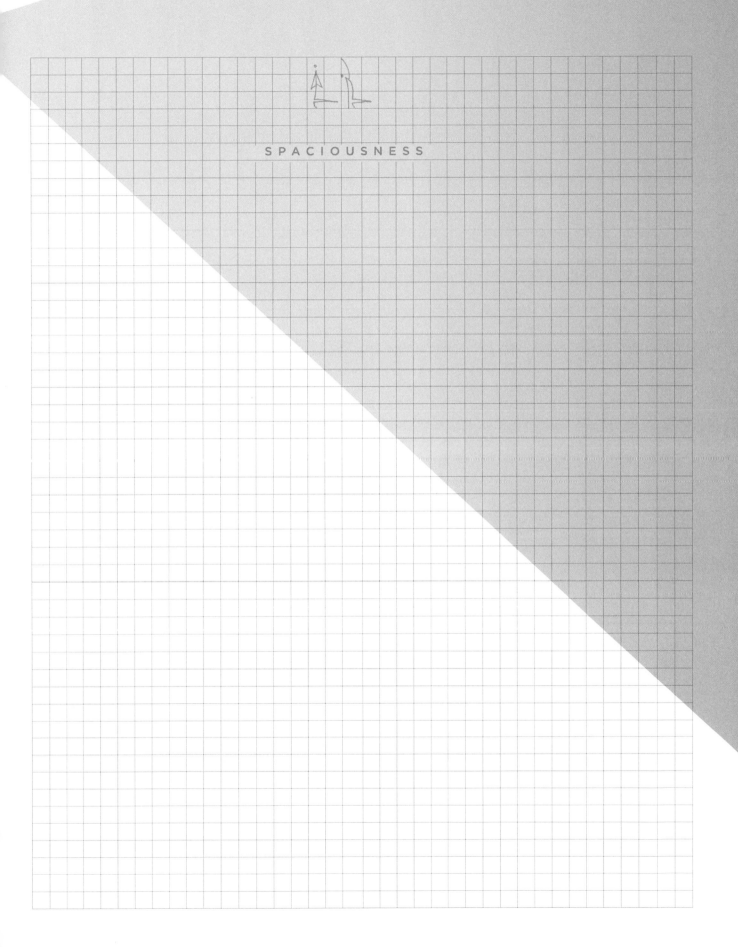

SPACIOUSNESS

TALKING POINTS

IT'S A MATTER OF
INNER ATTITUDE,
AND THE MERCILESS
DISCERNMENT OF
WHAT MOTIVATES US...

- R.S. DE LUBICZ

IT IS NOT NECESSARY
TO KEEP ONE'S MIND
COMPLETELY FREE
OF THOUGHTS AND
CONDITIONS IN ORDER
TO HEAL. WHAT IS
NECESSARY... TO SLOW
DOWN THE INTERNAL
DIALOGUE... THIS
WILL BE ENOUGH TO
PRODUCE A SPACE
IN WHICH WE CAN
REMAIN ALERT.

- GURUDEV SINGH

TALKING POINTS

THE GREATEST HIGH ON
EARTH IS BEING ABLE
TO TRUST YOURSELF.

- LAUREN ZANDER

YOU ARE ALWAYS HOME.

AIM: _____

WAVE ONE _____

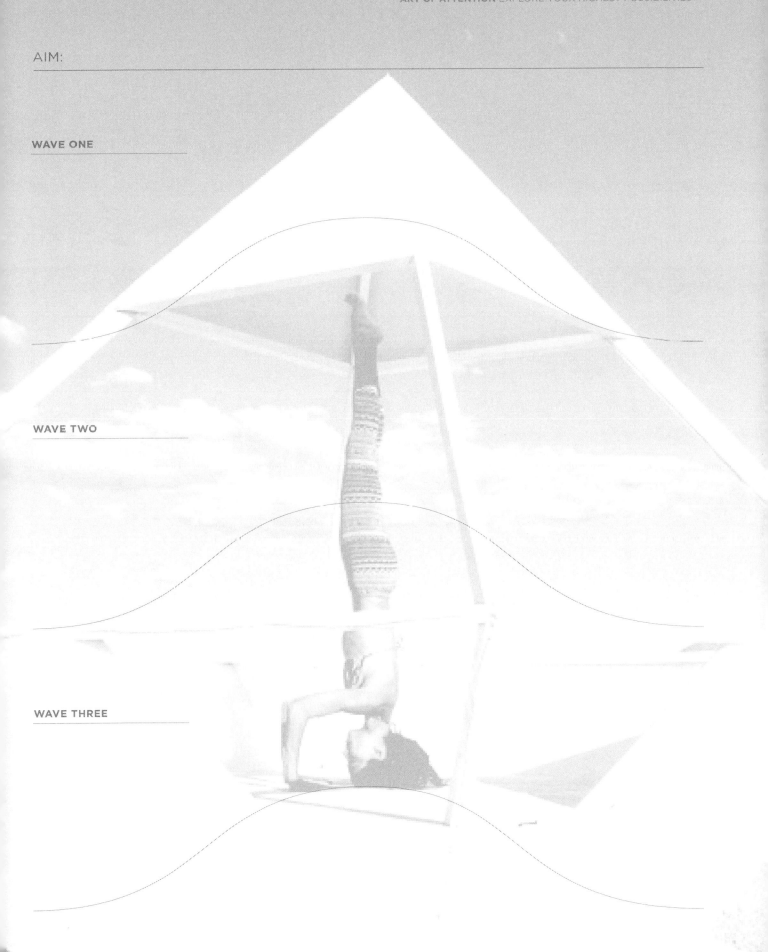

WAVE TWO _____

WAVE THREE _____

AWAKENING

YOUR HEART WORKS FOR YOU.
BUT DO YOU WORK FOR YOUR HEART?

- YOGI BHAJAN

WE SHOULD NEVER ALLOW FEARS OR
THE EXPECTATIONS OF OTHERS TO
SET THE FRONTIERS OF OUR DESTINY.

- ANAM CARA

CHRISTY TURLINGTON BURNS

THE BEAUTY OF A YOGA PRACTICE OR ANY LIFE PRACTICE IS THAT IT IS EVER EVOLVING, NEVER FIXED. There is always something to work on or toward. We don't work hard at these sorts of practices just to arrive at a goal, because it's in the practice that we find the fruits of our existence. Art of Attention provides a way for all of us to address the practice as the goal, and in this chapter, Let Your Life Reflect Your Practice, you'll find countless inspirations for creating sacred space, crafting sequences that lift you up and enjoying the journey of it all.

The practice itself doesn't have to be fixed either. For me, yoga has been a decades-long exploration of self, and that is what brought me closer to my current path as an advocate for global maternal health. To live a life of purpose has been a personal goal of mine for many years. Setting my attention on this intention allows me to see what could be perceived as obstacles in my life as opportunities to find connection or union with others. When I experienced a complication after delivering my first child, I became conscious of an issue that I knew nothing about, which soon became my focus. I learned that hundreds of thousands of women die from similar complications in pregnancy or childbirth all over the world, even though nearly all of them can be prevented with access to basic maternity care and information.

In 2010, I founded Every Mother Counts, an advocacy and mobilization campaign to increase education and support for maternal mortality reduction globally. EMC seeks to engage new audiences to better understand the challenges and solutions while encouraging them to take action to improve the lives of girls and women worldwide. I truly believe that together, we can make pregnancy and childbirth safe for all moms. This is my practice. May this chapter and this book help you define, refine and enjoy your own.

I truly believe that together we can make pregnancy and childbirth safe for all moms.

YOU ARE INVITED TO LET YOUR LIFE REFLECT YOUR PRACTICE.

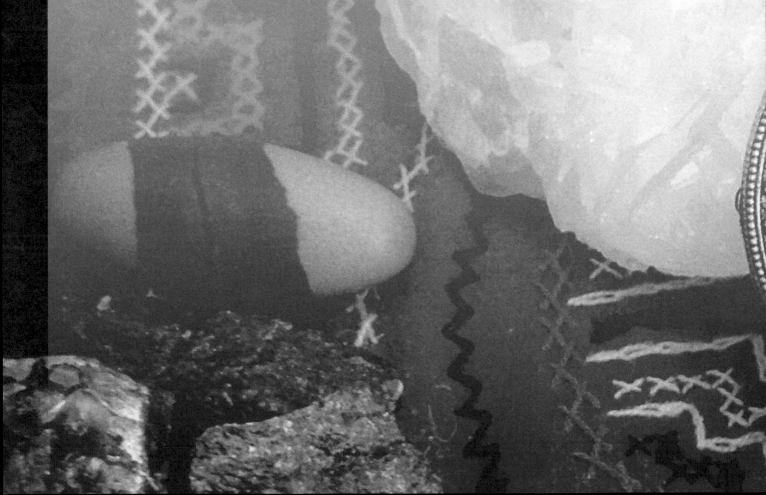

CHAPTER 5

LET YOUR LIFE REFLECT YOUR PRACTICE

photography by **DOMINIC NEITZ**

Practice as **PRASAD:** How you offer yourself in your practice mirrors how you're offering yourself in your life. Cultivate a refined perspective on how to create a quality of consistency and thoughtfulness, both in your body and in your relationships. Short standing pose flows, headstand, backbends and a sweet shavasana to integrate the consistent **EMANATION** both within and around you.

When
you offer
PRASAD, it represents the
submission, the opening to grace
which makes the exchange possible. You
can maintain protocol for years and never
really touch the esoteric level of this path, that is,
you can keep from getting into trouble. But once you
get serious the divine starts to get serious. You have to be
very sober about taking that one step because pretty soon you
will be stepping more quickly, but the divine will be running full
speed towards you.

– LEE LOZOWICK

SANKALPA

WELCOME. TAKE A COMFORTABLE SEAT.

Let your hands rest face down on your thighs; bring your index fingers and thumbs to touch. Close your eyes and settle into your breathing, into your body. Lean back a bit and sit deeply down onto your sitting bones. Inhale to lengthen up from your seat, up through the length of your neck, to the backs of your eyes. Exhale to sit taller.

Breathe deeply.

As we practice, we are offering ourselves up, completely. Not just our body, our resources, our minds, but everything. **PRASAD** is a metaphor for the **EXCHANGE** that takes place when we practice yoga. Any effort we make, in our practice or in our lives, is our prasad. We bring in information, we emanate understanding. While prasad is usually a sweet gift we offer to a teacher, with this practice we explore the quality of the offering we can make in any moment.

In our postures, we offer our effort as our **EMANATION** as we expand within the architecture of the pose. With this practice, we explore the quality of our effort in some poses. We see that it is all our choice. Rather than one big blast of energy that drains us, here we'll practice consistent, curative, conscious offering.

When we're relating to others, engaging in any way, instead of blasting our assumptions and draining ourselves, we can instead, with every glance, every gesture, every word, make a steady, stabilizing offering.

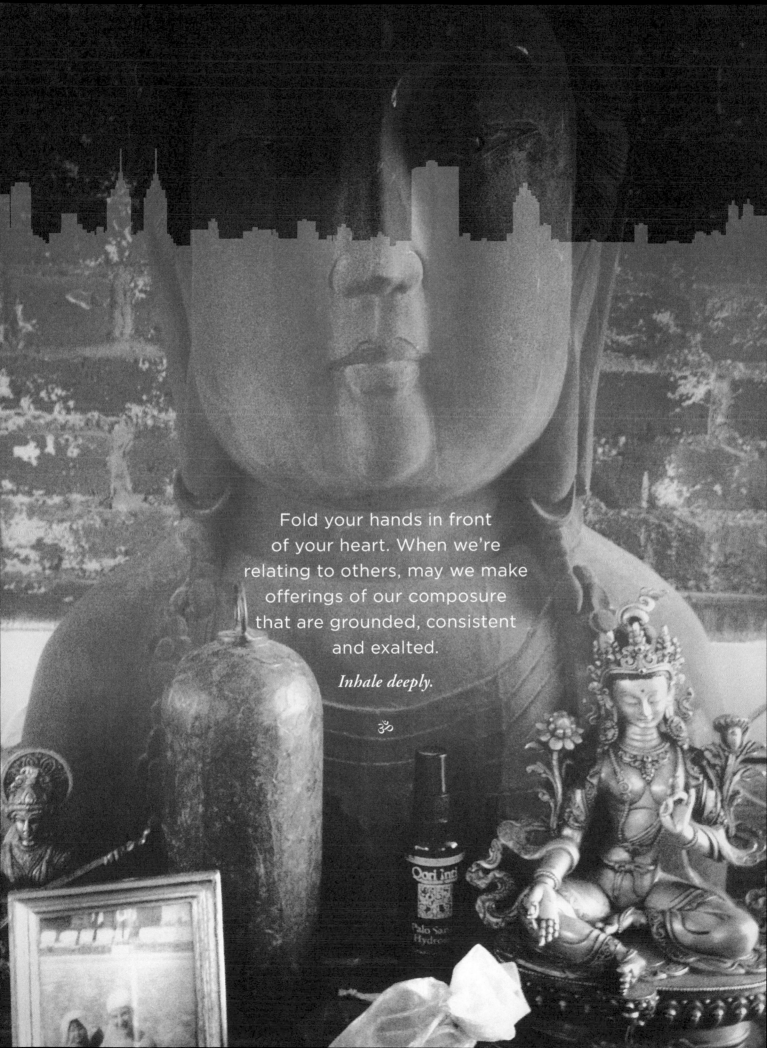

Fold your hands in front
of your heart. When we're
relating to others, may we make
offerings of our composure
that are grounded, consistent
and exalted.

Inhale deeply.

ॐ

LET YOUR LIFE REFLECT YOUR PRACTICE

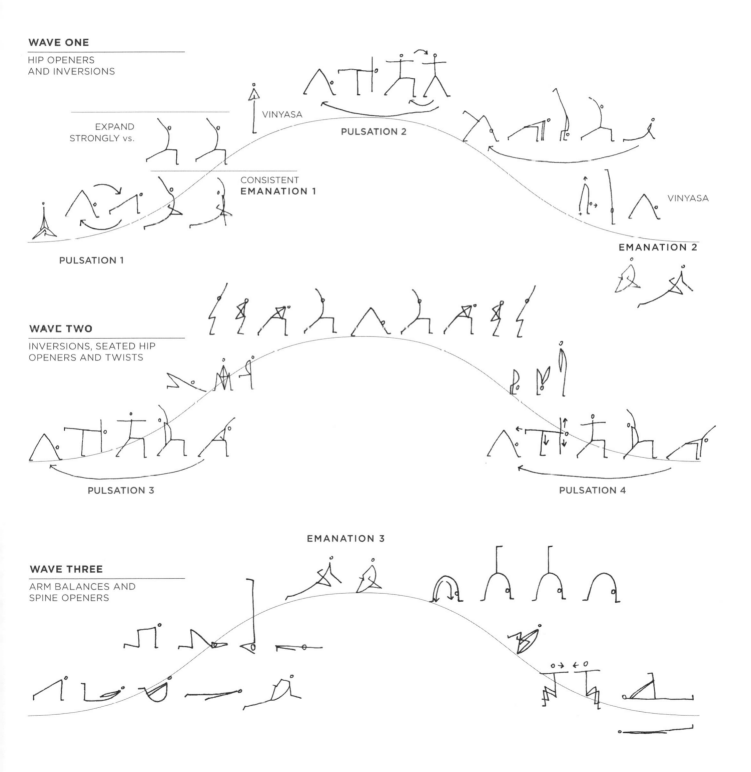

WAVE ONE

HIP OPENERS
AND INVERSIONS

VINYASA

EXPAND
STRONGLY vs.

PULSATION 2

CONSISTENT
EMANATION 1

VINYASA

EMANATION 2

PULSATION 1

WAVE TWO

INVERSIONS, SEATED HIP
OPENERS AND TWISTS

PULSATION 3

PULSATION 4

EMANATION 3

WAVE THREE

ARM BALANCES AND
SPINE OPENERS

PULSATION 1

PLANK POSE TO DOWNWARD FACING DOG

Beginning in Downward Facing Dog, claw the floor with your finger tips to energetically lift from your hands to your heart. From your heart extend generously down through your hands; press your heels back and straighten your legs forward into Plank Pose. Keep your legs strong.

Exhale back to Downward Facing Dog. Inhale forward to Plank Pose. Move back to Downward Facing Dog.

Consciously play with the speed of your movement; feel your body warming up, feel the length in your limbs. Take a few breaths back and forth until you're warm. Move back to Downward Facing Dog. From your heart, expand down through your hands for three to five breaths.

Emanate consistently
expand consciously

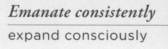

Explore every effort
how are you offering?

EXPAND STRONGLY VS. CONSISTENT EMANATION

EKA PADA RAJAKAPOTASANA
ONE-LEGGED KING PIGEON POSE

Bring your right knee forward for Pigeon Prep. Keep your back toes tucked; press out through your back heel. Walk your hands back until your fingertips are next to your hips, and you're sitting upright.

Hug your legs in from knee to knee, lift your pelvis, and lengthen from your waist to your heart, all the way up into your eyes. Soften your eyes.

Soften the sides of your neck and move your neck back in space. Keeping your legs strong, emanate out slowly, from your pelvis through both knees. Steadily lower your pelvis closer to the floor. Keeping your right hand on the floor, lift your left arm high. Again inhale, draw your knees in toward one another; exhale, emanate and lower gently. Now bring your right arm up, parallel to your left arm.

EXPERIMENT: From the floor of your pelvis, expand too strongly by "blasting" energy from the floor of your pelvis out to every peripheral point. Blast energetically through all four limbs into the room, as though clearing out your body.

Now to the more stable, consistent opening. Inhale to draw into the floor of your pelvis from every peripheral part, and, as you exhale slowly, open conscientiously and consistently for a slow, sweet **EMANATION** of energy. A steady release.

Take three to five breaths here.

Place your hands back down onto the floor; step back to Downward Facing Dog.

Left knee forward for Pigeon Prep. Keep your back toes tucked; reach back through your back heel. Walk your hands back until they're next to your hips. This is an exploration of any effort, and how it reveals itself in your body and your life. Left hand fingertips stay down. Raise your right arm high. Collect energy from knee to knee to lift energetically from the floor of your pelvis upward; through your heart, to your eyes - then soften your eyes.

Move your outer right hip towards the floor, then reach your left hand high, parallel to your right.

EXPERIMENT: From the floor of your pelvis, blast out into all four limbs - which can feel light and spacious. Then in contrast, emanate slowly, like a fire that gently and consistently warms, rather than burns.

Our aim is to be more conscious with how we share our energy in general; in poses and in our lives.

Bring hands to floor, step back to Downward Facing Dog.

EXPAND STRONGLY

CONSISTENT EMANATION

Often we find ourselves making efforts and offerings that we didn't intend to make. If we've consciously chosen to practice yoga it's time to recognize, consciously - whether it's a word, a glance, or an action - how we are offering ourselves to the world.

EXPAND STRONGLY VS. CONSISTENT EMANATION

ANJANEYASANA | HIGH LUNGE

One foot forward. Again, explore the difference: come into your Lunge and blast energy outward from your pelvic floor, in every direction. Make it a super-strong light-filled blast of energy. Take three to five breaths, come to Downward Facing Dog, and try your **SECOND SIDE**.

In doing this on our mats, we can see more clearly where our energetic leaks are in our interactions, our relationships. It may feel great in the moment, but we see that it takes more energy to blast than it does to be more thoughtful and consistent.

Plank Pose, Chaturanga Dandasana, Upward Facing Dog - let the back of your heart merge with the front of your heart - Downward Facing Dog.

How can we conserve emotional energy in our daily lives?

VI

TO BE CENTERED

SAME SIDE, SECOND TIME.

ANJANEYASANA | HIGH LUNGE

Come into your Lunge for the second time, same side.

Draw in from both feet to the floor of your pelvis, then emanate out consciously through all limbs. Make this a steady, consistent EMANATION. We are exploring how to conserve our energy in our daily lives as much as in our poses.

Take three to five breaths, SECOND SIDE.

So often we blast our words, gestures, actions from a place of doubt, worry, fear. Instead, can we consistently and softly assess and respond to what is really happening? This practice helps us turn away from perceived problems and stay steady in reality.

TADASANA WITH ANJALI MUDRA
MOUNTAIN POSE WITH HANDS TO HEART

Stand tall with your eyes closed. Feel in
your body what's resonating for you about
this exploration.

Do you typically fight - with others or with
yourself? This is a practice in which to explore
a consistent, steady awareness of what is. To
practice being magnificently supportive of
yourself, and learn to express yourself from a
very steady and sure space.

*Keep connected to your foundation; hands
to your mat. Plank Pose, Chaturanga
Dandasana, Upward Facing Dog. Exhale back
Downward Facing Dog.*

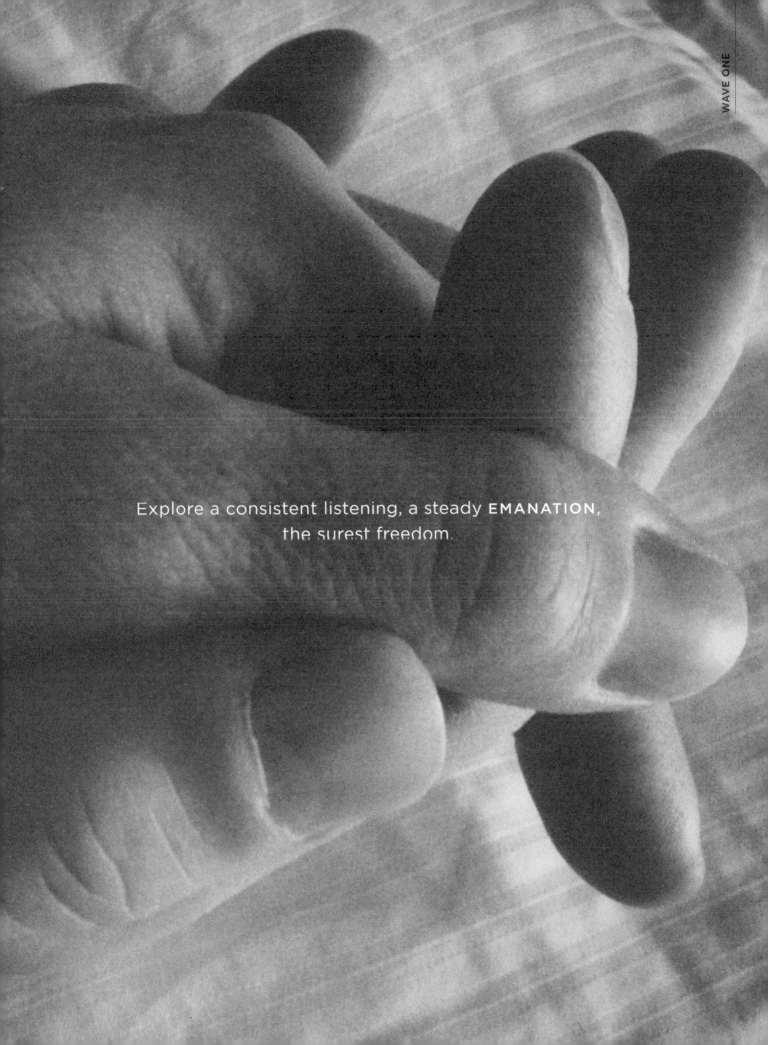

Explore a consistent listening, a steady **EMANATION**,
the surest freedom.

PULSATION 2

ARDHA CHANDRASANA | HALF MOON POSE
TO VIRABHADRASANA II | WARRIOR II

Come into Ardha Chandrasana, Half Moon Pose, on your right foot. Collect energy from every distal point into the floor of your pelvis and feel that strength in your body. From that point very consistently and with the same velocity and intensity in every limb, expand gently. Relax your toes.

Left hand down to left waist, keeping your left leg strong, slowly descend your back foot to the back of your mat for Warrior II. Bend your front knee deeply.

Inhale to hug in and straighten your front leg; exhale emanate evenly to bend your front knee.

Twice more, inhale to straighten your front leg, exhale to descend deeply into Warrior II. Once more.

Step back into Plank Pose, Chaturanga Dandasana, Upward Facing Dog, Downward Facing Dog.

Inhale gather energy
front leg straight

SECOND SIDE: Come into Ardha Chandrasana, Half Moon Pose, on your left foot; right foot flexed. From your pelvis, lengthen out consistently, in every direction, with consciousness and clarity. Move energy out through each limb with the same velocity and intensity.

Keep your back leg strong, bring your right hand to your right waist, reach back place your back foot down onto the back of your mat into Warrior II.

Inhale to lift up and draw your front leg straight. Exhale bend your front knee deeply, sink down evenly, emanate outward steadily. Again, inhale straighten your front leg; exhale, sink more deeply into Warrior II and expand evenly through the whole of your body.

LAST TIME: inhale hug in, and exhale still **LOWER** into Warrior II.

Exhale emanate steadily
bend front knee deeply

URDHVA PRASARITA EKA PADASANA
STANDING SPLITS
TO ANJANEYASANA
HIGH LUNGE

Step one foot forward to Standing Split, keep your top foot flexed, keep your hips square, lift and move your outer standing hip back, your outer standing thigh, outer knee, outer shin, outer baby toe back, to lift your top leg higher. Take the balance if you wish. Keep your velocity and intensity even in all your limbs. Lengthen your spine toward the floor through the top of your head. Exhale to lift your inner back thigh.

Release back slowly to High Lunge, arms up by your ears.

Keep the velocity and intensity even in all your limbs

CALM
SPACIOUS
ELEVATED
OPEN

AWAKE
IN LOVE
LISTENING
READY

PEACE

Teachers open the door, but you must enter by yourself.

"No one can listen to your body for you... To grow and heal, you have to take responsibility for listening to it yourself."
—Jon Kabat-Zinn

VINYASA

Emanating energy

evenly

Consider a current situation in which you are doing too much and draining your energy. In this pose, practice evenly emanating energy with that situation in your mind. On your mat, practice evenness internally to become more consistent in any context.

Throughout this vinyasa, from start to finish, emanate energy evenly.

Vinyasa to your SECOND SIDE.

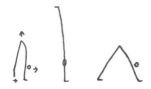

VRKSASANA
HANDSTAND

Walk your feet halfway forward, come up off your heels to the tips of your toes. Bring your heart forward over your hands. Lift your belly up high, bring gaze forward of your hands, your shoulders forward of your hands. **SMILE.** Consistently emanate. Come forward, raise your seat, breathing and smiling, seat now comes over your shoulders... **HIGHER**... one last breath.

Gently release.
Downward Facing Dog.

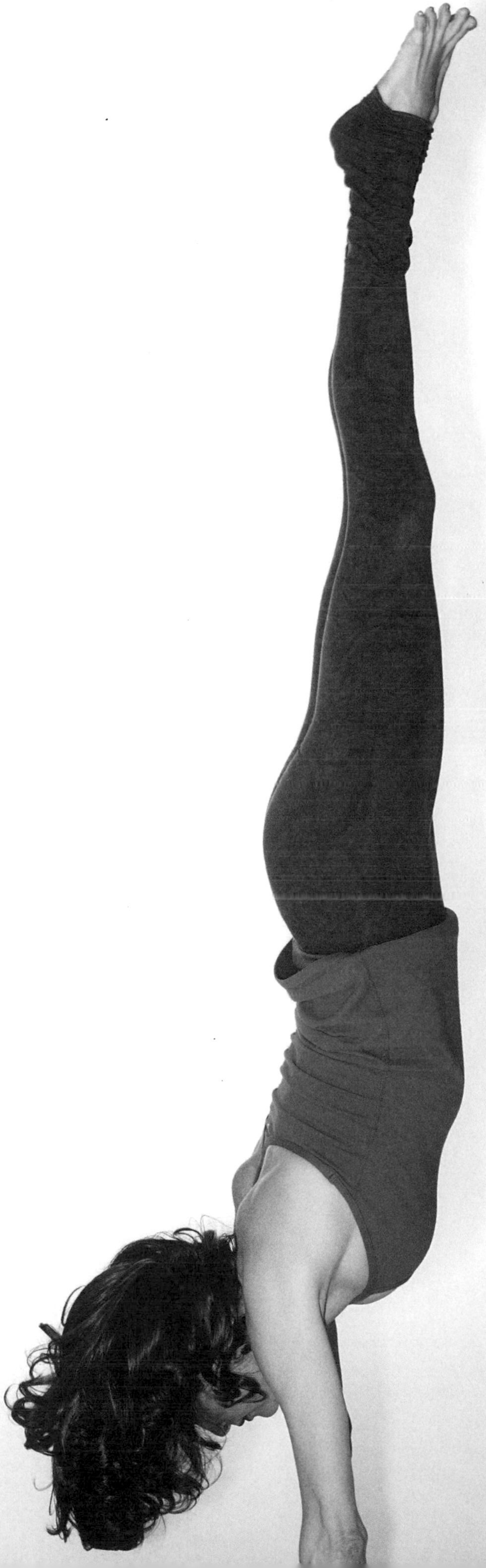

EMANATION 2

EKA PADA RAJAKAPOTASANA
ONE-LEGGED KING PIGEON POSE WITH
THIGH STRETCH

Right knee forward. bend your left knee and use your left hand to hold the inside of left foot for your thigh stretch. Place your right hand finger tips on the floor next to your right hip. Draw your left thigh up energetically towards your front heel, bring your back heel down towards your back seat.

Keep your left shoulderblade on your back, tail down, and spin your left hand fingers to face the same direction as your toes.

Open your back seat wide to the side and bring your left heel toward your seat. Walk your right hand onto your right thigh. From the floor of your pelvis, expand slowly through the whole of your body. Keep broadening your left seat, and reach your right seat back and down. SMILE. Move the sides of your neck back.

Notice any energetic inconsistencies (one place is tight while the other is full of oxygen, for example). Emanate thoughtfully and consistently in every direction from the floor of your pelvis. Let that consistency inform your behavior with everyone; let it determine how you hold your gaze and the muscles of your face.

Take three to five breaths there. Gently release to come down to your elbows. Downward Facing Dog.

SECOND SIDE: Left knee forward. bend your right knee; hold the inside of your right foot with your right hand. Place your left hand finger tips on the floor next to your left hip. Draw your right knee energetically towards your front heel. Bring your back heel down towards your back seat.

Keep your right shoulderblade on your back and spin your right hand fingers to face the same direction as your toes.

Open your back seat wide as you bring your heel down. Walk your left hand onto your left thigh; emanate slowly out. Keep broadening your right seat, left seat back and down.

Take three to five breaths, then come down onto your elbows.

We're cultivating an offering that is warming and nourishing - not consuming. We can be more consistent in how we share and offer our energy. We can stay more connected to the ease that is always available.

With this exploration we cultivate a connectedness
that has nothing to do with tension at all.
Vanda Scaravelli writes, *"Tension is a theft."* For us to
practice consistency in the way in which we offer our
energy is to eliminate that theft from our lives.

THIS IS A DAILY EFFORT - our worry and doubt

steal our energy, creating tension in the body.
Yoga helps us be more consistent in how we communicate
in any arena.

The Book of Questions

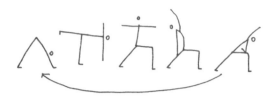

PULSATION 3

ARDHA CHANDRASANA | HALF MOON

Expand from the floor of your pelvis in every direction evenly and consistently. Notice which limbs get more attention; practice being consistent and even here, in every direction.

VIRABHADRASANA II | WARRIOR II

Root down through your back foot to bend your front knee more deeply. Locate where you aren't present and consistently emanate energy there.

Throughout your being
consistent EMANATION

VIPARITA VIRABHADRASANA II
REVERSE WARRIOR II

See where your energy is pooling; expand it more evenly throughout. Keep emanating out consistently, in every direction.

UTTHITA PARSVAKONASANA | SIDE ANGLE

Compare your two feet - can you be more consistent with the weight in each foot? As you collect the energy from your feet to your core, can you redistribute it evenly throughout your body?

Move back into Downward Facing Dog.

MALASANA | YOGI SQUAT TO
BAKASANA | CROW

Press down into your feet, press your knees out against your elbows, and lift tall through the back of your heart. Close your eyes and feel the steadiness that comes with this consistency as you breathe for a moment.

Place your knees onto your elbows for Crow Pose. Inhale to hug in, bend your elbows - exhale to lift your feet, straighten your arms and lift your back body. Inhale bend your elbows to get low; exhale jump back to Chaturanga Dandasana, Upward Facing Dog, Downward Facing Dog.

Each day is very different in our bodies. We can practice noticing where energy is blocked, and how we can use this practice of consistent **EMANATION** to even out the way in which we offer ourselves in any pose or in anything we do.

We stay young through cultivation of this awareness.

PARIVRITTA UTKATASANA WITH ANJALI MUDRA | CHAIR TWIST WITH HANDS TO HEART **TO** PARIVRITTA ANJANEYASANA WITH ANJALI MUDRA | HIGH LUNGE TWIST WITH HANDS TO HEART

From Tadasana, bend your knees into Chair Pose. Lower your hands to prayer, twist to one side, make sure your knees and hips are even and parallel. Emanate throughout your limbs evenly; notice the softening in your face, your forehead, your third eye.

Hold spacious and steady, and step your opposite foot to the back of your mat.

Press your hands gently into prayer. Spin your bottom belly to top belly, expand from your pelvis into every direction evenly. Find a slight backbend here.

Hands down; Plank Pose, Chaturanga Dandasana, Upward Facing Dog, Downward Facing Dog.

Step your second foot forward, come to High Lunge, hands in prayer, twist to the second side; breathe consistently throughout the pose. Then step your back foot up to Chair, your knees and hips parallel.

Inhale tall to stand, and exhale fold.

UTTANASANA | STANDING FORWARD FOLD WITH HANDS INTERLACED **TO** TADASANA | MOUNTAIN POSE

Interlace your arms behind you, and expand evenly throughout your body. Allow the opening to reach perimeter parts of you that you rarely access. Allow your shoulderblades to move toward the back of your heart; open your heart in this even, balanced way. Strong legs, inhale come to stand. Exhale hands down at your sides; palms facing forward.

Sense the sweet ease in your body here.

Every time we balance ourselves interiorly in this way, even during a conversation, there is a shift - in us and in the people near us.

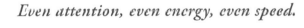

PULSATION 4
LAST TIME, BOTH SIDES.

HALF MOON | WARRIOR II | REVERSE
WARRIOR | SIDE ANGLE POSE

Everyday, we have situations during which we
wish for more elegance. In the movement from
Half Moon to Warrior II, focus on keeping the
consistency of your interior opening to cultivate
elegance through this transition.

Maintain balanced **EMANATION** throughout
your limbs.

When we're about to reach maximum
expenditure in any pose or moment, may we be
more consistent with how we share our energy.

Even attention, even energy, even speed.

May we be consistent
and elegant
in our offerings

BELLY TO THE FLOOR

DHANURASANA | UPWARD BOW

Bend your knees so your feet face the ceiling. Interlace your hands behind you. Keep your knees parallel, lengthen your tailbone towards the back of your mat. Keep your hands interlaced; bend your elbows to lift your shoulderblades away from the floor. Lengthen your tailbone toward the back of your mat even more. Keeping your hands interlaced, use your hands to root your tailbone back toward your knees as you lift your upper body gently away from the floor. Rather than blasting out, maintain this balanced **EMANATION** as you breathe.

This is a great approximation of any difficult moment. We can practice facing the situation without wasting or draining our energy.

Reach back to take your feet with your hands now.

Draw more attention to the floor of your pelvis; stay on the soft part of your belly. Soften your eyes.

Emanate throughout your body with each exhalation.

Now lift your feet high into Bow Pose. Root your tailbone down even more towards the floor, move the back of your throat softly back in space for three to five breaths.

Gently release. Rest your head to one side; relax.

Too often our outer posture is not representing our inner posture, our external behavior isn't matching what we're thinking or feeling and that conflict drains us.

Explore bringing consistency to both your inward stance and your outer posture.

May we bring
consistency

ARDHA BHEKASANA | HALF FROG POSE

Forehead to the floor.

Bring your left arm in front of you, forearm across the front of your chest on the floor. Prop yourself up on your left elbow. Bend your right knee and place your right hand to the top of your right foot; ensure the right knee is parallel to your left. As you bring your heel toward your seat, widen your seat. Keep your right shoulderblade on your back, fingers facing the same direction as the toes.

Close your eyes, inhale to collect energy from your feet into the floor of your pelvis; make your **EMANATION** even through every part of your body as you extend your legs for a few breaths.

Exhale to sense the difference from your left to right side; create symmetry internally and externally.

Let your head rest on your hands; feel your body's response.

SECOND SIDE: Right forearm across you, left hand to left foot. As you arrange the pose on this side, widen your seat, draw your left foot closer to your outer hip and inhale to gently collect your energy in. Every time you exhale, evenly expand out.

Put your attention on your highest self, and inhabit that space every time you come to your mat. Make every offering exactly what you choose.

Make your slow steady offering of this pose
this moment

SIRSASANA | HEADSTAND

Prop yourself up on both elbows and interlace your hands. Tuck your bottom pinky into your hands. Place the top of your head on the floor in front of your thumbs, keeping your hands closely interlaced, and rest the back of your head against the meaty parts of your thumbs. Do not open your hands to cradle your head; keeping your hands closed is safest for your neck and spine. Tuck your toes, lift knees and walk your feet in. Create a consistent **EMANATION** in your body. Draw in from your arms energetically to the top of your head, and expand out through the rest of your body, slowly and steadily. Whether you come up to balance today is secondary - are you emanating energy consistently throughout your body? Let this consistency stabilize you.

Enjoy the pose for about a minute, or as long as you wish.

Maintain energetic consistency and speed as you lower down
with straight legs
if you can

BALASANA |
CHILD'S POSE WITH
FULL PRANAAM

Feel the response
of your body; the
interior opening.

*Gently return to
your Downward
Facing Dog.*

EMANATION 3

EKA PADA RAJAKAPOTASANA
ONE-LEGGED TWISTED PIGEON POSE

Right knee forward, come down onto your left forearm, bend your left knee and take hold of the little toe side of your left foot with your right hand. Open your toes, close your eyes, and notice where most of your energy is pooling. Invite your attention and energy into the floor of your pelvis. From there, expand in every direction evenly, slowly, consistently, until you find your way back into the backbend. Spine long, allow the back of your heart to merge with the front of your heart, even front to back, right to left. Legs, arms - everything - even **EMANATION**. Feel that balance in your face and eyes.

Take several breaths there, and then release and rest on both elbows for a few breaths. Return to Downward Facing Dog.

SECOND SIDE: Left knee forward to pigeon, right forearm down, bend your right knee and take a hold of the outer edge of your right foot with your left hand. Feel where you are situated in your body, where most of your attention is pooling, and then gather it into the floor of your pelvis and expand out evenly, patiently, consistently into your backbend here. Every exhalation is another vista, another offering, another gift.

Release, and rest on your elbows for a few breaths. Exhale back to Downward Facing Dog, forward to Plank Pose, Chaturanga Dandasana, to your belly, to roll over onto your back.

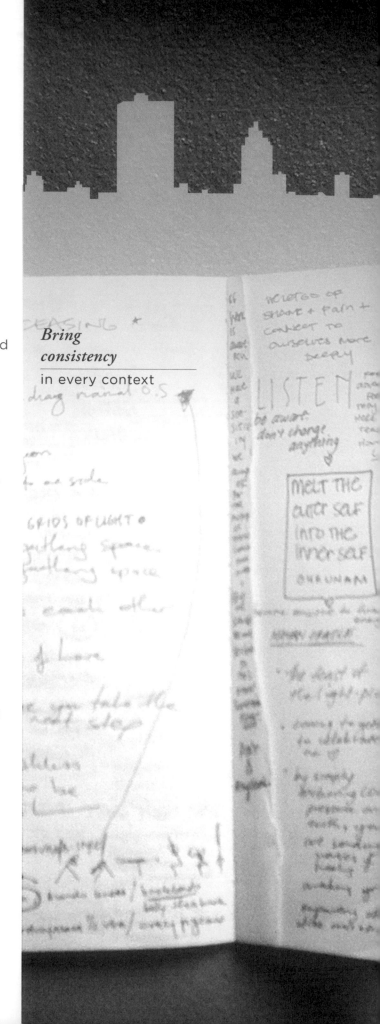

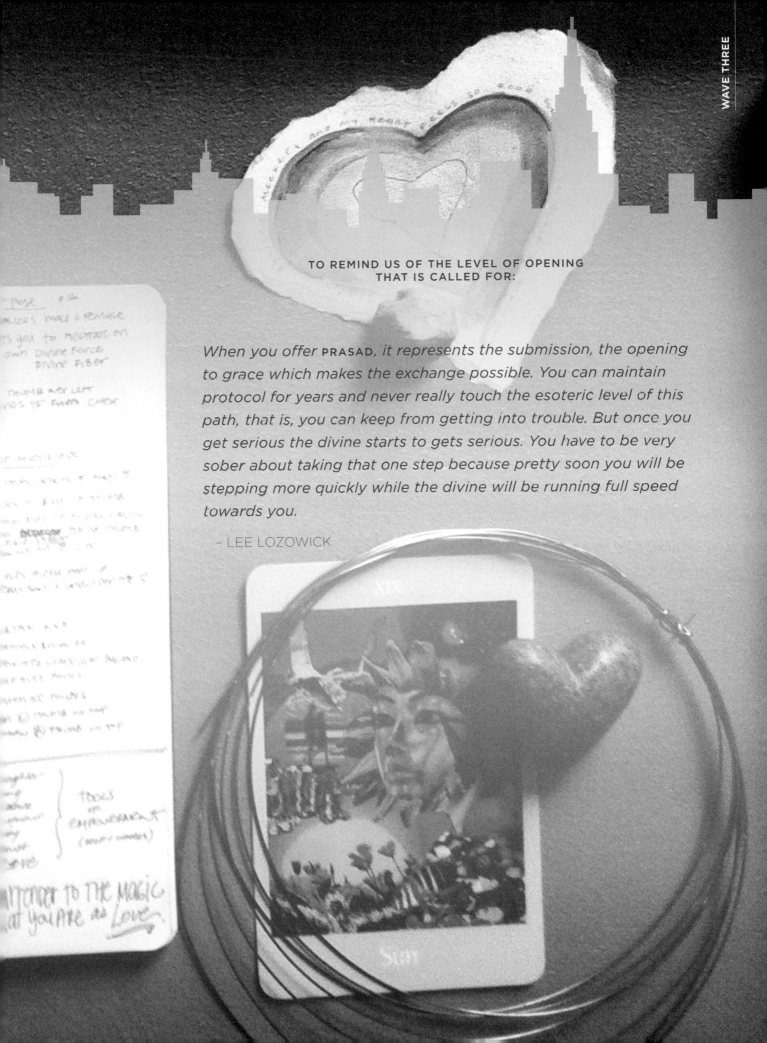

**TO REMIND US OF THE LEVEL OF OPENING
THAT IS CALLED FOR:**

When you offer PRASAD, *it represents the submission, the opening
to grace which makes the exchange possible. You can maintain
protocol for years and never really touch the esoteric level of this
path, that is, you can keep from getting into trouble. But once you
get serious the divine starts to gets serious. You have to be very
sober about taking that one step because pretty soon you will be
stepping more quickly while the divine will be running full speed
towards you.*

– LEE LOZOWICK

THREADING THE NEEDLE

Roll over onto your back, bend your knees and place your feet on the floor hip-width apart. Bring your right ankle on top of left knee and thread your right arm through your legs, interlace your hands either behind your left thigh or on top of your left shin. Widen your right seat away from you as you bring your right knee closer to you.

Pause.

Then bend your elbows to draw your left knee closer to you, place your shoulderblades on the floor and flex both feet strongly. Notice where your attention is pooling, draw more energy into your hips, then gently open out - evenly, consistently, thoughtfully. Move your right knee away now to increase the intensity, and practice an even **EMANATION** outward from your hips. Draw your left knee even closer, maintaining the consistency of the **EMANATION**. Gently release, lengthen your legs long onto the floor and feel your body's response. Lengthen the back of your neck and rest, listening, for a few moments.

Switch sides and enjoy.

Bring your left ankle on top of your right knee and thread your left arm through, then interlace hands behind your right thigh or on top of your right shin. Widen your left seat away from you and bring that left knee closer to you.

Pause.

Bend your elbows to draw your right knee closer now; shoulderblades to the floor. Flex both feet strongly. Draw into the floor of your pelvis; then gently expand thoughtfully outward. Your practice is your offering of consistency. Maintaining the consistency of the **EMANATION**, draw your right knee closer now, then gently release. Lengthen your legs long on the floor and feel the response for several breaths.

Bend your knees to place both feet on the floor.

Your practice
is your offering of consistency

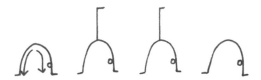

URDHVA DHANURASANA | FULL WHEEL

Place your hands next to your ears, just beneath your shoulders. Root your feet down. Gather energy into the floor of your pelvis; create a thoughtful **EMANATION** outward. Every exhalation is a chance to open thoughtfully, sweetly, steadily. Come up to the top of your head, draw your hands and feet towards one another, lift your head away from floor, shoulderblades towards your heart. Then expand to rise up; lengthen your knees and arms straight, and lift your head.

Expand down from your hips through your hands and feet, evenly. Lengthen and straighten all four limbs, evenly and slowly. When we patiently expand interiorly, we experience more endurance.

Breathe two breaths, then slowly look up to lower down.

May we bring thoughtful softness and consistency
through our practice
into our lives

SECOND TIME

URDHVA DHANURASANA | FULL WHEEL

For your second wheel, come all the way up, open your limbs evenly. Bring your right knee into your chest, then straighten that leg high to the sky. Root your standing inner thigh energetically down and emanate through your right and left legs evenly.

We are always being asked to address some unexpected asymmetry: How do we cultivate consistency in any context?

THIRD TIME

URDHVA DHANURASANA | FULL WHEEL

Come on up. Once you're up, bring your left knee into your chest, then straighten that leg long; notice any imbalance, any insecurity, and then even things out, both structurally and internally.

Expand every limb thoughtfully and consistently.

FOURTH AND FINAL

URDHVA DHANURASANA | FULL WHEEL

Last time, super grounded, feet and hands evenly weighted for a few breaths. Come on down when you're ready, and lengthen your legs out long.

JATHARA PARIVARTANASANA | SUPINE SPINAL TWIST

Extend your arms out to the sides like a "T" and let your knees fall casually to your left. In daily situations, begin to see where you've drained your energy by automatically letting your attention dwell unintentionally, and place it with intent on your breathing.

Breathe here for at least a minute, then switch sides.

SUPTA PADANGUSTHASANA | RECLINED LEG STRETCH

Lengthen your left leg long on the floor; straighten your right leg up towards the sky. Interlace your hands behind your right hamstring, close to your groin. Root both thighbones away from you and reset your **EMANATION** in this form so that everything is evenly open. Soften your face, and your eyes.

Take five to ten breaths there, then switch sides.

SHAVASANA
CORPSE

Close your eyes when you're ready. As you settle in, lengthen the back of your neck long, let your shoulderblades descend to the floor.

Place your right hand on your belly, your left hand on your heart.

Healing
internal recalibration awaits

Today, how can I make an
offering that is even, thoughtful,
consistent, balanced?

AWAKENING

Notice the stillness, the evenness in your body.

Begin to deepen your breathing.

In all we do, may we consistently refine how we offer ourselves.

Bring your knees into your chest.

Roll to your right side and come up to sitting.

Rest your hands on your thighs for a couple of moments, eyes closed. Sit back onto your sitting bones, shift your heart until it's on top of your seat, allow your neck to gently rest on top of your heart, and your head to rest on top of your spine.

To put our attention on how we are **EMANATING** in these poses is a healing act.

Fold your hands in front of your heart.

In each of our interactions and relationships, may we offer our attention with elegant consistency.

To your presence, to your capacity to be honest about where you are standing and where you're going in everything you do.

To all of our teachers.

NAMASTE.

SANKALPA

THE IMPORTANT THING IS WHAT WE DO
DURING AN ACTIVE NEGATIVE STATE,
NOT JUST WHEN WE ARE READING AND
CONTEMPLATING SPIRITUAL BOOKS OR
LISTENING TO A DHARMA TALK.

- PETER RHODES

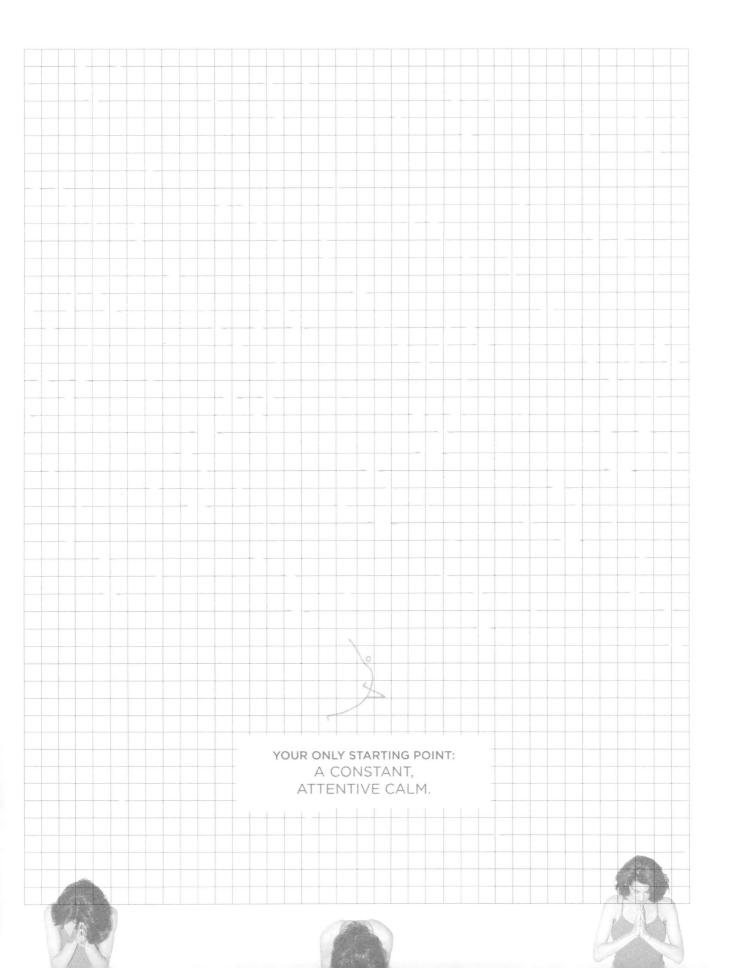

YOUR ONLY STARTING POINT:
A CONSTANT,
ATTENTIVE CALM.

TALKING POINTS

SPIRITUAL WORK IS THE
TRAINING OF THE MIND SO
THAT IT CAN REACH WITHIN
AND BEYOND OUR CHEMISTRY
TO BRING ABOUT THE
SITUATION THAT WE WANT.

- RUDI

WE MAKE A MISTAKE WHEN
WE WAIT FOR HEAVEN,
WAIT FOR ENLIGHTENMENT,
WAIT FOR CHANGE.
IT IS NOT GOING TO HAPPEN
IN THE FUTURE. IT *IS* HAPPENING.
IT IS WITHIN OUR EXPERIENCE.
NOW IS THE TIME.

- PETER RHODES

TALKING POINTS

WE ARE SO CONDITIONED TO BELIEVE
THAT WHEN WE SEE A PROBLEM WE MUST
IMMEDIATELY FIX IT, THAT ONE OF THE MOST
DIFFICULT THINGS TO DO IN THIS WORK IS TO
OBSERVE WITHOUT INTERFERENCE, NEITHER
JUDGING NOR CHANGING WHAT IS OBSERVED.
LAY DOWN YOUR SWORD AND
CEASE FIGHTING, WEARY TRAVELER.
TO FIGHT IS A TRAP.

- RED HAWK

YOU ARE ALWAYS HOME.

AIM:

WAVE ONE

WAVE TWO

WAVE THREE

AWAKENING

...THE MORE INNER WORK IS DEEPENED,
THE WIDER EXTERNAL WORK SHOULD
BECOME, AND THE MORE EXTERNAL
WORK WIDENS, THE DEEPER INTERNAL
WORK SHOULD BECOME.

- RODNEY COLLIN

HEALING IS THE REMEMBRANCE
OF YOUR WHOLENESS.

- DEEPAK CHOPRA

ACKNOWLEDGMENTS

Thank you Erica Jago for being a light, a wing, and a source. I am honoured to be presenting this alongside you.

Thank you Mimi and Papa, Anthony and Jonah Lyon, Jessie, Jeff and Cory Nichols, Bentley and Jensen Meeker, Lyn Nelson, Leila Astarabadi, Alexandra Lyon Perelman, Jonathan, Will and Jackson Perelman, Papa T Lyon, Judith Lyon, Shannon Port and Kate Thorson for my magical family. And to Chloe Crespi, Betty Kay Kendrick, Raja Sethuraman and the team at Gloss Studios NYC, Dominic Neitz, Michael Chichi, Alice Marshall, Gregg Greenwood, Kristen Lotto, Garth Stevenson, Yves Durif and Julia March, I give thanks to you for ensuring the beauty.

Thank you Linda Sparrowe for editing our project! You were instrumental, and we are humbled.

Thank you to the teachers and staff of VIRAYOGA. Kiri Binihaky and Karen McCulloch, Glenna Bedoya and especially Lynn Hazan.

Thank you to the Zander family, the Weissenberger family, the Nir family, Laurie Gerber, Will Craig, Hildie Dunn, Samantha Sutton, Linda Colletta, and Katie Torpey for the love, for the teachings, the contact with the truth, and for giving me my family back.

For your style, guidance, love and encouragement throughout the years, thank you Dr. Douglas Brooks, Louise Amar, Cyndi Lee, Rodney Yee and Colleen Saidman Yee, Seane Corn, Alison West, Dana Flynn, Mark Whitwell, Alejandro Junger, Hugo Cory, J. Brown, Vinnie Marino, Douglas Drummond, Rebecca Dreyfus, Suzannah Ludwig, Sensei John Mirrione and the Harmony by Karate family, John Friend, Marlo Phillips, Erin Boucher Kennedy, Liz Eustace, Melissa Eustace, Ally Bogard, Meghan Currie, Sianna Sherman, Janet Stone, Sally Kempton, Saul David Raye, Shiva Rea, Bryan Kest, Erich Schiffman, Desiree Rumbaugh, Beryl Bender Birch, Leslie Kaminoff, Schuyler Grant and the staff of Kula yoga, Marc Holzman, Anne Vandewalle, Gregoire Pothion, Marie Marty Lozach and the family at BeYoga Paris, Rusty Wells and the staff of Urban Flow Yoga, Brook and Harrison Altman, Katie Hess of Lotus Wei, Lisa Reinhardt of Wei of Chocolate, Nadine Johnson, Mary Margrill, Lori Goldstein, Lysa Cooper, Athena, Victor and Jivan Calderone, Mads Kornerup, Daniel Cook, Danny Kalatsky, Gary Sheva, Eric Cahan, Katey Denno, Brock and Krista Cahill, Eva Mendes, Liev Schreiber, Naomi Watts, Russell Simmons, Zofia Reno, Peter Krause, Cristina Ehrlich, Dana Bauer, Judy Bauer, Sarah Perlis, Susan Cianciolo, Libby and Scooter Weintraub, Mijanou Montealagre and Michael Rothman, Kathryn Budig, Tiffany Cruikshank, MB LaRue, Mary Ellen Bonifati McGeough, Tali Magal and Craig Fleishman, Amir Magal, AK Kennedy, Hyde Yoga, Kira Ryder, Kaitlin Quistgaard, Richard Rosen, Scott Blossom, Bruno Danto, Gabriella and the Becchina family, Lole, Manduka, Kripalu, Omega Institute, the family at Growing Heart Farm, Anna Walko, Niki Morrisette, Jeff Krasno, Sean Hoess, Karina Mackenzie and the Wanderlust Festival, Stephanie Snyder, Kira Ryder and LuluBandha's, Amy Ippoliti, Christy and Gavin Mackenzie, Kia Miller, Tommy Rosen, Ashley Turner, Mark Mangan and Sascha Lewis.

Thank you Ekyog and Only Hearts for wardrobe in Chapter One. Thank you Jin Seo of 51inc, Leila Astarabadi, Lululemon and kd dance for wardrobe, and Yael Alkalay's red flower for candles in Chapter Two. Thank you B by Donna M for wardrobe in Chapter Three. Thank you Jin Seo of 51inc for wardrobe in Chapter Four. Thank you Lululemon and Victoria Keen for wardrobe, Nadia Narain for candles, Plank Designs for a perfect mat, Jamie Young for our precious murti, Qori Inti for divine Palo Santo mist, Karuna Malas for my beloved mala, and Mother Earth for the crystals in Chapter Five.

Thank you Pam Katch for your work on the first Art of Attention project, that gave way to this one.

Thank you Derik, Ryan and the YogaGlo family for the incredible opening you've provided in the sharing of the practice, and for being the seed for this project.

Thank you especially to Mark Roemer, David Kennedy, Nikki Costello, Christina Sell, Darren and Peter Rhodes, Jill Miller, MC Yogi, Gabrielle Bernstein, Donna Karan, Gwyneth Paltrow Martin, Christy Turlington Burns, Dr. Mark Hyman, Tara Stiles, Kaitlin Quistgaard, Dr. Frank Lipman, Kris Carr, Latham Thomas, Brian and Alexandra Jaye Johnson, and Bentley Meeker for being an integral part of what's led to this book, and to all of the students who've graced my path. Thank you.

ERICA WOULD LIKE TO THANK: Elena for bringing me into my heart and expanding my capacity for love. Michael Chichi for being a catalyst; always encouraging me to be the artist that I am. My inspiring family of support: Dee Dee and Nick Lloyd, Duane, Beth and Kaci Jago, Brooke, Jesse, Ella and Swing Mullins, Jared Thear, Dorothy Jago, Mary and Bob Leeper, Janie Triplet and Family, Bo Powell and Family, Amanda Dates, Joanna Intara Zim and the Durga Divas, Deborah Horwith, Taryn Lynch, Jennifer Frances and Steven Lichtscheidl, Luc, Kristyn and Stella Pritchett, Dave Bull, Nansee Parker, Julie Howard, San Francisco, Amsterdam and Hawaii's Women Yoga Groups, Robert Dupper, Dominika Swietlik, Charle Marais, Marianne de Kuyper, Nina Beatty, Andrea Stern, Jenna Hann, Ryan Gamlin and Krisha Fairchild. Love you all.

TOGETHER, ELENA AND ERICA WOULD LIKE TO THANK: Michael ChiChi, Harlan Emil, Sofia Escobar, Chloe Crespi, Raja Sethuraman, Kristen Lotto, Dominic Neitz, Alice Marshall, Linda Sparrowe, Sally Kempton, Diana Krebs, Maren Brand, Kamphausen, Bérénice von Bandel, Emily Mattoon, John Kohler and Rachel Perlman at Gloss Studios, the teachers and staff of Urban Flow SF, BeYoga Paris, and Satori Yoga Studio, Burning Man, Camera Girl, Marian Goodell, Mike Bradley, Tommy Bolduc, Elise Gochberg, Yves Durif and The Carlyle, A Rosewood Hotel.

REDUCE TENSION AND FIND FORGIVENESS

CHAPTER ONE POSE SEQUENCE

TADASANA | MOUNTAIN POSE

SURYA NAMASKARA A | SUN SALUTATION

UTKATASANA | CHAIR

VIRABHADRASANA II | WARRIOR II

UTTHITA PARSVAKONASANA | SIDE ANGLE

UTTHITA TRIKONASANA | TRIANGLE

ASHVA SANCHALANASANA | GALLOPING HORSE

ONE MIN HOLD — ADHO MUKHA SHVANASANA | DOWNWARD FACING DOG

UTTANASANA | STANDING FORWARD FOLD TO HANUMANASANA | SPLITS

URDHVA PRASARITA EKA PADASANA | STANDING SPLITS TO ADHO MUKHA SHVANASANA | DOWNWARD FACING DOG

PARIVRITTA ANJANEYASANA WITH ANJALI MUDRA | HIGH LUNGE TWIST WITH HANDS TO HEART

UTKATASANA | CHAIR TO UTTANASANA | STANDING FORWARD FOLD WITH HANDS INTERLACED

 ONE MIN HOLD

ADHO MUKHA SHVANASANA | DOWNWARD FACING DOG

VRKSASANA | HANDSTAND

PARIVRITTA ANJANEYASANA | HIGH LUNGE TWIST

BAKASANA | CROW

SECOND TIME: HANUMANASANA | SPLITS

ONE MIN HOLD

ADHO MUKHA SHVANASANA | DOWNWARD FACING DOG

DOWNWARD FACING DOG > PLANK POSE > UPWARD FACING DOG > COBRA > LOCUST

DHANURASANA | UPWARD BOW

SUPTA TADASANA | RECLINED MOUNTAIN

URDHVA DHANURASANA | FULL WHEEL

SUPTA PADANGUSTHASANA | RECLINED LEG STRETCH

SHAVASANA | CORPSE

LET GO OF BLAME

CHAPTER TWO POSE SEQUENCE

SNAPSHOT
Can you feel more resonance?

feet together

URDHVA BADDHA HASTASANA | UPWARD BOUND HAND POSE

TWIST L/R

PRASARITA PADOTTANASANA | WIDE-LEGGED FORWARD BEND

SNAPSHOT
Are you present right now?

BADDHA VIRABHADRASANA | HUMBLE WARRIOR

SNAPSHOT
Can you be there for yourself?

SOLAR PLEXUS

top of the mat

SURYA NAMASKARA A | SUN SALUTATION

jump to seated

PASCHIMOTTANASANA | SEATED FORWARD BEND

SNAPSHOT
Can you be more sweet?

use prop if rounded back

PURVOTTANASANA | UPWARD PLANK POSE

SOLES OF FEET pressing into one another

BADDHA KONASANA | BOUND ANGLE

PALMS FACING UP
seat on the floor

ACTIVATE. RELEASE
facial muscles

SUPTA BADDHA KONASANA | RECLINED BOUND ANGLE

TWIST L/R
knees to one side, gaze to the other side

JATHARA PARIVARTANASANA | SUPINE SPINAL TWIST

Virasana options

OPTION 2
seat on floor

OPTION 1
seat on prop

OPTION 3
fully reclined, seat on floor

VIRASANA | HERO POSE

 gaze L/R

BALASANA | CHILD'S POSE

DOWN DOG
head resting on prop

RESTORATIVE ADHO MUKHA SHVANASANA | DOWNWARD FACING DOG

CHILD'S POSE
prop to navel

RESTORATIVE BALASANA | CHILD'S POSE

PROP UNDER SACRUM
seat against wall

VIPARITA KARANI | LEGS UP THE WALL

Shavasana options

OPTION 2
sit bones on the floor

OPTION 1
shoulders on the floor

OPTION 3
sit bones on the floor

SHAVASANA | CORPSE POSE

SNAPSHOT
Take a full impression of your entire being

CHAPTER THREE

BREATHE AND FIND STILLNESS

EXPLORE YOUR HIGHEST POSSIBILITIES

CHAPTER FOUR POSE SEQUENCE

SHOULDER ALIGNMENT

1 Lengthen both sides of your body long.

2 Bring the heads of your arm bones back.

3 Gently press the bottom tips of your shoulderblades into the back of your heart.

4 Energetically turn your forearms in and your upper arms out.

5 Expand that entire form from the inside out.

EXHALE opening
INHALE rounding

CAT/COW POSE

ADHO MUKHA SHVANASANA | DOWNWARD FACING DOG WITH BENT KNEES

BRING YOUR AWARENESS to that space

PARIVRITTA ANJANEYASANA | HIGH LUNGE TWIST

UTTHITA TRIKONASANA | TRIANGLE

VIRABHADRASANA II | WARRIOR II **TO** VIPARITA VIRABHADRASANA | REVERSE WARRIOR

FILL YOURSELF with space

PRASARITA PADOTTANASANA | WIDE-LEGGED FORWARD BEND WITH HANDS INTERLACED **TO** **TADASANA** | MOUNTAIN POSE

UTTHITA PARSVAKONASANA | SIDE ANGLE

VIRABHADRASANA I | WARRIOR I

VASISTHASANA VARIATION | SIDE PLANK POSE WITH SLIGHT BACKBEND

BALASANA | CHILD'S POSE

EKA PADA RAJAKAPOTASANA | ONE-LEGGED KING PIGEON POSE

EXTEND WILLINGNESS in all you do

JANU SIRSASANA | HEAD-TO-KNEE FORWARD BEND

UPAVISTHA KONASANA | WIDE-LEGGED SEATED FORWARD BEND

BHARADVAJASANA II | HALF SEATED TWIST

PARSVA BAKASANA / DVI PADA KOUNDINYASANA | SIDE CROW POSE BREAKDOWN

SIDDHASANA / SUKHASANA | SEATED

SETU BANDHASANA TO URDHVA DHANURASANA | BRIDGE TO FULL WHEEL

ANY SITUATION hold it in front of you

JATHARA PARIVARTANASANA | SUPINE SPINAL TWIST

RE-ROOT THIGHS

SERVING your family, friends, work

SHAVASANA | CORPSE

LET YOUR LIFE REFLECT YOUR PRACTICE

CHAPTER FIVE POSE SEQUENCE

PULSATION 1  PLANK POSE TO
DOWNWARD FACING DOG

CONSISTENT
EMANATION 1 EKA PADA
RAJAKAPOTASANA |
ONE-LEGGED KING
PIGEON POSE

PARIVRITTA UTKATASANA WITH ANJALI MUDRA
| CHAIR TWIST WITH HANDS TO HEART **TO**
PARIVRITTA ANJANEYASANA WITH ANJALI MUDRA
| HIGH LUNGE TWIST WITH HANDS TO HEART

EXPAND
STRONGLY vs. ANJANEYASANA | HIGH
LUNGE

VINYASA TADASANA WITH ANJALI
MUDRA | MOUNTAIN POSE
WITH HANDS TO HEART

UTTANASANA | STANDING
FORWARD FOLD WITH
HANDS INTERLACED
TO TADASANA |
MOUNTAIN POSE

PULSATION 2  ARDHA CHANDRASANA
| HALF MOON POSE **TO**
VIRABHADRASANA II |
WARRIOR II

HALF MOON | WARRIOR II
| REVERSE WARRIOR |
SIDE ANGLE POSE

PULSATION 4

 URDHVA PRASARITA
EKA PADASANA |
STANDING SPLITS **TO**
ANJANEYASANA | HIGH
LUNGE

DHANURASANA |
UPWARD BOW

ARDHA BHEKASANA |
HALF FROG POSE

VRKSASANA |
HANDSTAND

SIRSASANA | HEADSTAND

VINYASA

EMANATION 2 EKA PADA
RAJAKAPOTASANA |
ONE-LEGGED KING
PIGEON POSE **WITH**
THIGH STRETCH

EMANATION 3 EKA PADA
RAJAKAPOTASANA |
ONE-LEGGED TWISTED
PIGEON POSE

 THREADING THE NEEDLE

 ARDHA CHANDRASANA
| HALF MOON **TO**
VIRABHADRASANA II |
WARRIOR II TO VIPARITA
VIRABHADRASANA II |
REVERSE WARRIOR
II TO UTTHITA
PARSVAKONASANA |
SIDE ANGLE

PULSATION 3

URDHVA DHANURASANA |
FULL WHEEL

 JATHARA
PARIVARTANASANA |
SUPINE SPINAL TWIST

SUPTA
PADANGUSTHASANA |
RECLINED LEG STRETCH

 MALASANA |
YOGI SQUAT **TO**
BAKASANA | CROW

 SHAVASANA | CORPSE